Art Is a Powerful Language

Willard Hirsch—The Man, The Artist

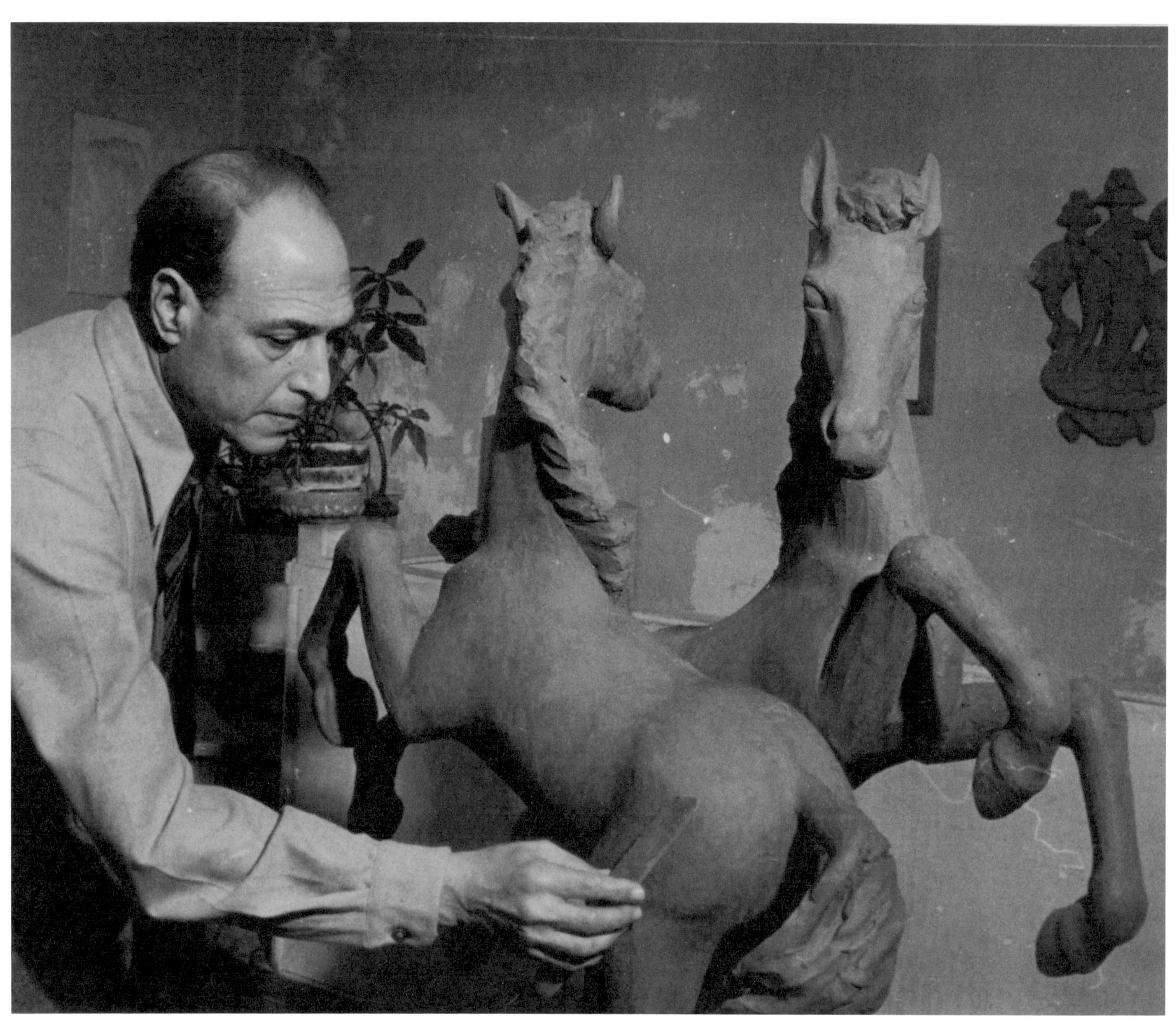

Willard Hirsch working on his *Prancing Colts*, 1959. Photo by Louis Schwartz.

Art Is a Powerful Language

Willard Hirsch—The Man, The Artist

Compiled by Jane Elizabeth Hirsch
Photography by Douglas M. Pinkerton
Edited by Amy Fluet

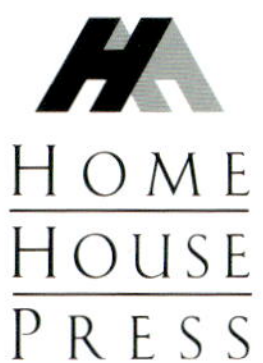

CHARLESTON, SOUTH CAROLINA

Published by Home House Press
109 Broad Street
Charleston, SC 29401
HomeHousePress@gmail.com
www.homehousepress.org

Designed by Paul F. Rossmann

Printed by Thomson-Shore, Dexter, Michigan
First printing
ISBN 978-0-9845580-4-9

Cover Art: All images are by Willard Hirsch

Front Cover:
Background: *Readers*, 1961. Stainless steel, 6 ft. 4 wide in. X 4 ft. 8 in. tall, Charleston County Public Library, Charleston, S.C. Photo by Douglas M. Pinkerton.
Joy of Motherhood, 1970. Bronze, 11½ ft. long X 7½ ft. tall. Brookgreen Gardens, Murrells Inlet, S.C. Photo by Douglas M. Pinkerton.
My Family, 1957. Terra-cotta, 14 in. wide X 17 ½ in. tall, Hirsch family collection. Photo by Douglas M. Pinkerton.
Owl, n.d. Steel, 21 in. tall, Walterboro bank. Photo by Louis Schwartz.
Falling Angel, 1980. Bronze, 22 in. tall, Gibbes Museum of Art, Charleston, S.C. Photo by Douglas M. Pinkerton.
Alligator *wall fountain*, n.d. Terra-cotta, 23 in. tall, private collection. Hirsch family collection:
Chinese Boy, late 1930s. Terra-cotta, 9¾ in. tall X 9 in. wide, private collection. Photo by Douglas M. Pinkerton.
Cassique of Kiawah, 1971-72. Bronze, 8½ ft. tall, Charlestowne Landing, Charleston, S.C. Photo by Douglas M. Pinkerton.

Back cover:
Little Dancer, 1950s. Bronze, 22 in. tall, White Point Garden, Charleston, S.C. Photo by Douglas M. Pinkerton.
Dancing Angels, 1967. Terra-cotta, 15 in. tall, Hirsch family collection. Photo by Douglas M. Pinkerton.
Maternity #4. Terra-cotta, 7 in. tall, Hirsch family collection. Photo by Douglas M. Pinkerton.
Jacob's Dream, 1949. Planewood, 27 in. tall, Columbia Museum of Art, Columbia, S.C. Photo by Louis Schwartz.
Laura Bragg, 1969. Terra-cotta, 13 in. tall X 10 in. wide X 9 in. deep, Gibbes Museum of Art, Charleston, S.C. Photo by Louis Schwartz.

Endpapers: *Bear Family*, n.d. Terra-cotta, 20 in. tall, Office of the Bureau of Child Guidance, New York City. Photo by Louis Schwartz.

"Art is a language and a powerful one.
All of us should know at least a few words of it...."

— Willard Hirsch in a lecture to the Citadel Corps,
February 26, 1945

Dedication

In honor of my mother, Mordenai Hirsch, sparkling jewel of all jewels.
In memory of my father, Willard Hirsch, brilliant diamond in the rough.

— Jane Elizabeth Hirsch

ACKNOWLEDGMENTS

Although this work began as my idea, its growth and development were nourished by many people. The personal side of Daddy's story could not have been told without the support and input from my family: my mother, Mordenai Hirsch; my aunt, Rachel Raisin; my brother, Jack Hirsch; and my aunt, Ruth Hirsch.

The contributors—my mother, my brother, Martha R. Severens, Anne Worsham Richardson, Katherine Muschick Schneider, Thomas E. Thornhill, Harlan Greene, and Joseph Harrison—have provided unique insights into my father as an artist and teacher through their individual memories, which give my account greater depth.

Anyone who looks through this book will see that the beautiful photographs of my father's work are an integral part of telling his story. Ida Schwartz, whose husband Louis documented many of Daddy's pieces, generously gave me permission to use his photographs. In addition, I will always be indebted to Douglas M. Pinkerton for his expertise and for the vast amount of time that he dedicated to capturing the magnificence of Daddy's sculptures.

I am very grateful to Amy Fluet for her patient guidance and editing. Special thanks go to the Special Collections Department at the Marlene and Nathan Addlestone Library of the College of Charleston, including Dale Rosengarten, Marie Ferrara, and Harlan Greene, all of whom have encouraged, supported, guided, and assisted me in many ways from the very beginning. Their enthusiasm and trust gave me the courage to persevere.

And to Thomas Tisdale, Stephen Hoffius, and Home House Press: Thank you for having the courage to take on my book!

– Jane Elizabeth Hirsch

CONTENTS

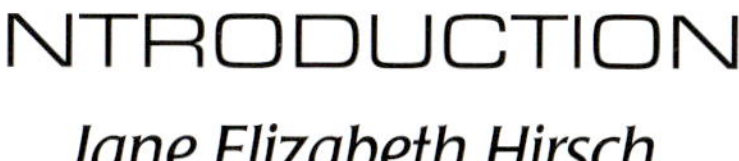

INTRODUCTION

Jane Elizabeth Hirsch

For several years, I have mulled over the idea of writing a book about my father, Willard Hirsch, the sculptor. As Charleston has grown and changed, many residents today know little or nothing about him, even though they might be familiar with some of his works around town.

An obituary from the *Columbia* (S.C.) *Record*, published December 13, 1982, reads, "Willard Newman Hirsch died the other day. Outside of his native Charleston, his passing received nowhere near the recognition it should have. He was a sculptor and teacher, an artist of no mean accomplishment and integrity...."

I hope that this book will provide a glimpse, seen through the eyes of family, friends, and colleagues, into one of Charleston's natives, who not only made a name for himself in the art world but also stood out as a colorful local character.

Writing this book has been a wonderful journey, winding and wading through the many memories of being Willard Hirsch's family, a mixture of laughter and love, some embarrassment and frustration, but above all a feeling of pride at having been a part of the life of such an amazing talent and person. He was one of a kind—a man proud of his work, outspoken about his beliefs, with an integrity rarely seen today, and a kindness that his family and friends remember lovingly.

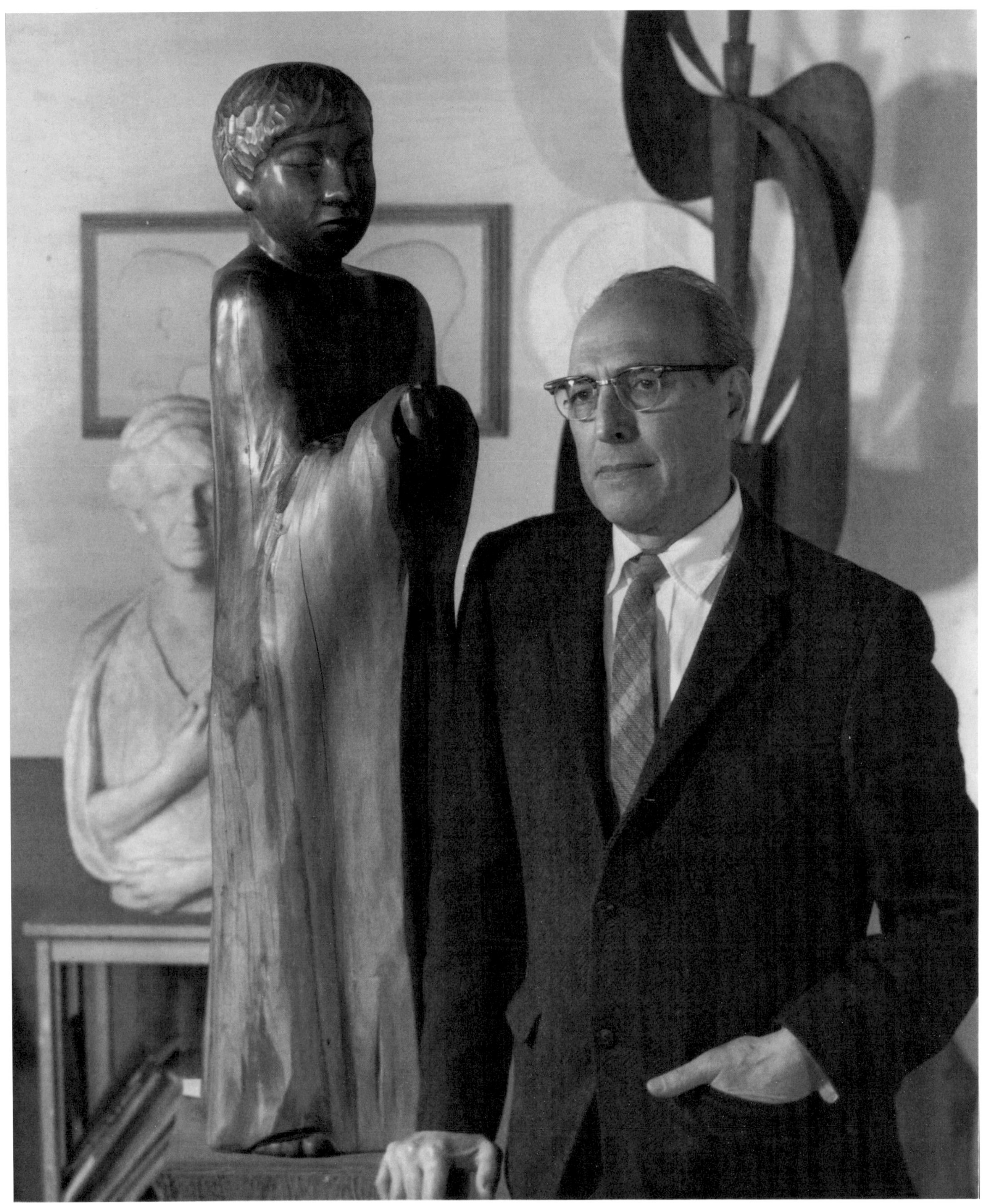

Fig. 1. Willard Hirsch with his *The Boy Joseph*. Photo by Louis J. Schwartz. The carved wood sculpture (1967, 44" x 14" x 10½") is among the collections of the South Carolina Arts Commission.

Willard Hirsch: Versatile, Imaginative, Creative

Martha R. Severens

A native of Charleston, Willard Newman Hirsch (1905-1982) elected to pursue sculpture, a medium that rarely received much patronage in the city of his birth. Nevertheless, Hirsch became a distinctive artist who made a successful career from private and public commissions, emerging as Charleston's premier sculptor of the twentieth century. He was versatile in both his subject matter and his ability to work in a variety of media, ranging from terra-cotta and plaster to wood and metal. In addition, he was a revered teacher and became a force in local art education.

Growing up on Montagu Street downtown, Hirsch attended local schools and the College of Charleston, but exactly when he developed an interest in art, and specifically sculpture, is unclear. He would have had few artists to emulate or sculptural models to inspire him. In the 1910s and early 1920s, the Charleston Renaissance was just getting underway, spearheaded by two artists, Alice Ravenel Huger Smith and Elizabeth O'Neill Verner. The former worked on several publications about the city's architectural legacy that were illustrated with her drawings, and those writings have been credited with inspiring the nascent preservation movement. Her protégé and cohort Verner was also interested in historic preservation. They each learned the intricacies of printmaking, and both were active in the Charleston Etchers' Club. Verner excelled in etchings, as did her rival Alfred Hutty—an outsider who made Charleston his winter home in 1920. Smith gradually abandoned prints in favor of watercolors, which she rendered loosely in a romantic style heavily influenced by Japanese art. None of these artists was inclined to mentor young artists or have students; William Halsey, who as a youth shadowed Verner on the streets of Charleston, was the one exception.

Hirsch probably had little awareness or contact with this circle of artists, which was dominated by women. In addition, they worked in two dimensions, mostly prints and watercolors, with an occasional oil painting. Around the city there was little sculpture to observe, with the exception of public monuments like Joseph Wilton's statue of William Pitt which graced Washington Square *(Figure 2)*, and the collection of marble portrait busts and plaques in City Hall. While the Gibbes Art Gallery hosted changing exhibitions from time to time,

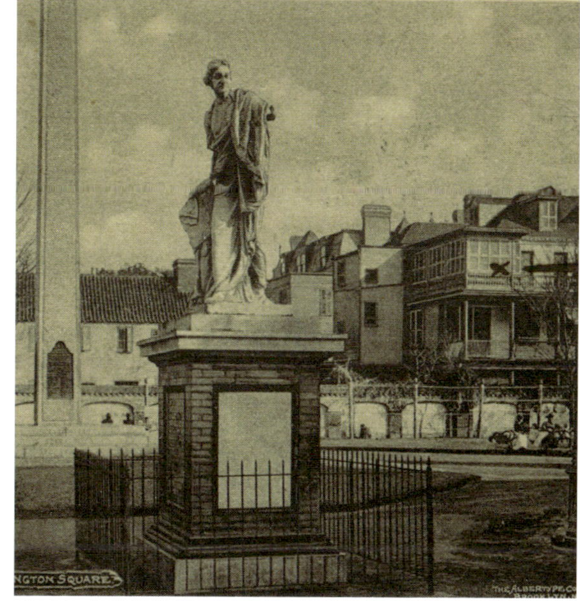

Fig. 2. Postcard of William Pitt Statue, Washington Square Park, Charleston, S.C., 1906. Courtesy of the South Caroliniana Library, University of South Carolina, Columbia. The sculpture, first erected in Charleston in 1767, now stands in the Charleston County Judicial Center.

the selections tended to feature paintings. How, and why, Hirsch, a descendant of a Jewish family that had been in the Lowcountry for generations, became a sculptor is veiled in mystery. The earliest documented display of interest occurred after he went to New York, when his aunt noticed him molding small objects from candle wax.

Fortunately for Hirsch, his aunt also offered to pay his tuition at the historic and distinguished National Academy of Design. Later he was awarded scholarships for some of its classes, which were taught by members. Located on Amsterdam Avenue and 109th Street, the academy was conventional in its teaching, emphasizing drawing from nude models and plaster casts. Here, between 1934 and 1937, Hirsch learned the fundamentals of art and met other aspiring artists. In 1935 he supplemented his studies at the Beaux Arts Institute, which had been established in 1916 to provide education and training for architects, and also for sculptors and muralists who would work on architectural commissions. The institution was founded during a national building boom that continued for several decades. Many of the buildings called for sculptural decoration for interior public spaces, as well as for their ever-taller towers.

Fig. 3. Study for theatre decoration with Abraham Lincoln theme, n.d. Photo from Hirsch family collection.

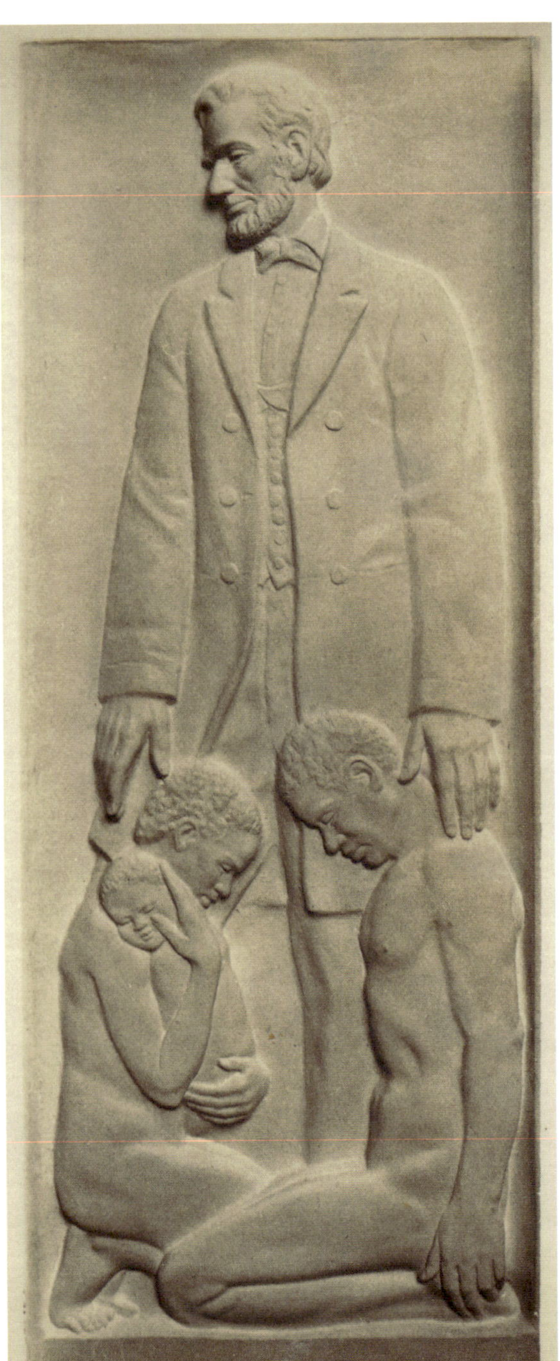

Few examples of Hirsch's work from this period are extant, although he was diligent in having photographs taken on a regular basis—a commendable trait that persisted throughout his life. These show mainly plaster models of female figures, both young and old, with robust, full-bodied proportions, in the manner of Aristide Maillol, a French classicist who was much admired by the academic community. Hirsch also undertook some reliefs with such historical themes as pilgrims, Indians, and Abraham Lincoln *(Figure 3)*, possibly for commissions that did not come to fruition. He exhibited regularly at the National Academy during his time in New York, although he was never invited to become an academician, an honor perhaps thwarted by the advent of World War II.

Although he was in his late thirties and suffered a hearing loss, Hirsch signed up with the United States Army, and served from 1942 to 1944. He was stationed at Fort Jackson, near Columbia, a mere one hundred and twenty miles from home. After the war, he decided to give up his New York studio and return to Charleston, where he would make a bigger impression—sort of the big fish in the small pond, an analogy he would have appreciated given his lifelong passion for fish and aquaria.

Charleston had changed since his departure over ten years before. Despite the Depression, the Lowcountry had experienced a surge in tourism, fueled by the artists of the Charleston Renaissance; hotels opened, garden and house tours took place every spring, and books were written celebrating the particular charms of "America's Most Historic City." Many artists, such as Smith, Verner, and Hutty, were making a living from their art. An historic-preservation ordinance—the first in the country—assured that large areas of the city would be immune from insensitive development. World War II brought thousands of soldiers and sailors, and their families, to the area, especially to an expanded Charleston Naval Base. For the first time since the antebellum period, Charleston's economy was thriving.

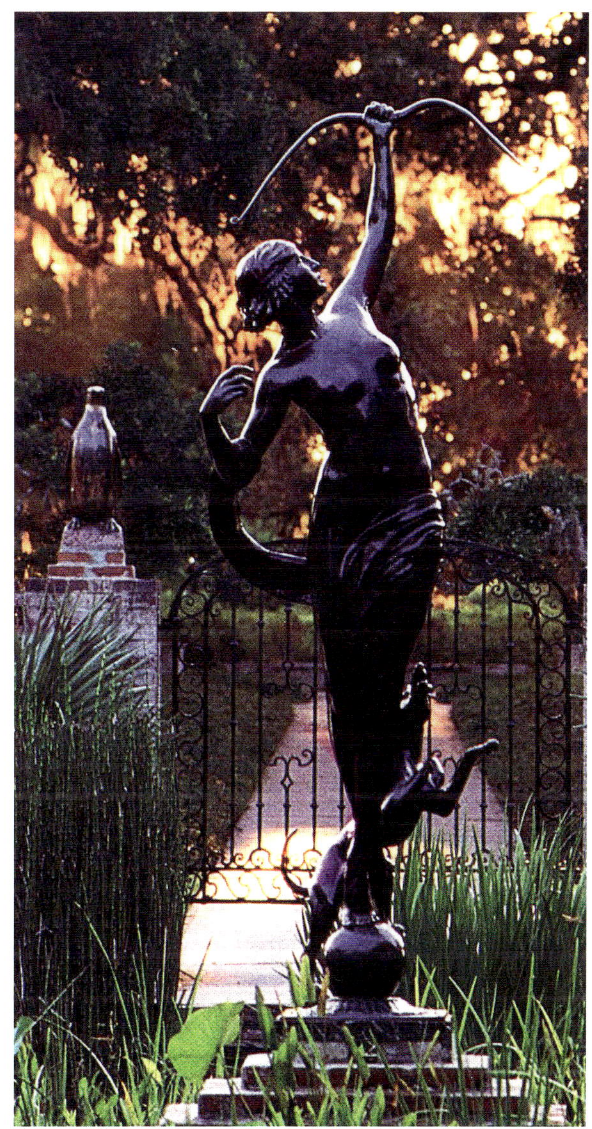

Fig. 4. Anna Hyatt Huntington (1876-1973), *Diana of the Chase*, 1922. Bronze, Brookgreen Gardens, Murrells Inlet, S.C. Photo courtesy of Brookgreen Gardens.

Seventy-five miles up the coast a unique and forward-looking attraction opened in Murrells Inlet as a showcase for American figurative sculpture: Brookgreen Gardens. The enlightened vision of railroad heir Archer M. Huntington and his wife, noted sculptor Anna Vaughn Hyatt Huntington, Brookgreen Gardens consisted of four former rice plantations, which the Huntingtons transformed into a sculpture garden. The mission of Brookgreen Gardens was, and still is, to preserve flora and fauna and display sculpture in a natural setting. The Huntingtons began acquiring sculpture and by the mid-1930s had installed an impressive collection of pieces by well-known sculptors. The taste was decidedly conservative and the themes often allegorical or heroic, much in line with Hirsch's predilections. Some were monumental in scale, such as Huntington's own *Diana of the Chase* at eight feet *(Figure 4)* and Paul Manship's gilded seven-foot bronze *Actaeon*. They were complemented by smaller works crafted by some of the instructors at the Beaux Arts Institute: Robert Aitken, John Gregory, Anthony de Francisi, and Gleb W. Derujinsky, all of whom worked in a classicizing mode.

When he returned to South Carolina, Hirsch reconnected with his roots. He soon opened a studio at 17 Exchange Street, and in 1945 built Charleston's first kiln for casting plaster and terra-cotta. He soon married Mordenai Raisin, the daughter of a venerated rabbi, solidifying further his commitment to succeed in his native city. In February 1945 he delivered a lecture at The Citadel, and his introduction demonstrates his sense of humor: "During my past two years in the army I was asked many times what I did in civilian life. I enjoyed the look of bewilderment that my answer, that I was a sculptor, brought to the faces of my questioners. There is widespread belief in the country, not prevalent here I know, that sculpture was an art of ancient Greece and that all the sculptors died out when Greece fell. I'm the living proof that such is not the case."[1]

Having broken the ice, he continued in a more caustic tone: "Sculpture is a vital living art in America, despite the apathy of the public and the indifference of the architects." He sought to explain this dilemma by stating: "Sculpture is cumbersome and expensive to exhibit." He cited the fact that because art schools were located

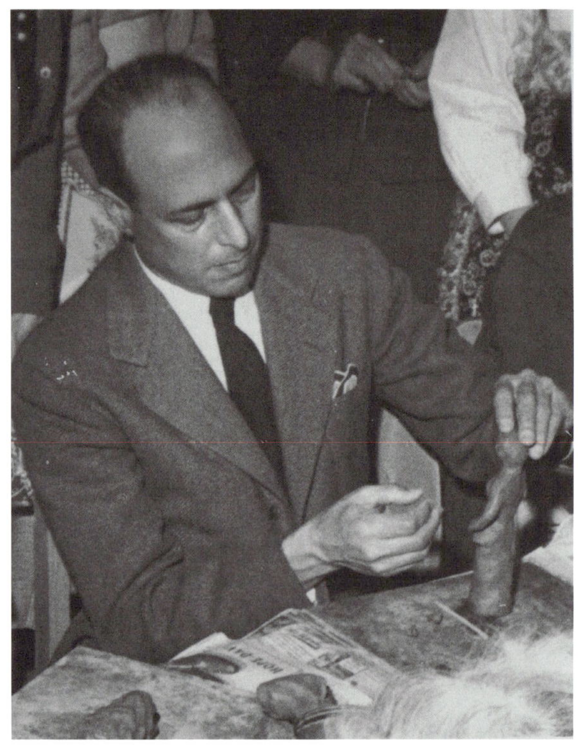

Fig. 5. Willard Hirsch, about 1950. Hirsch family collection.

only in large metropolitan areas, artists tended to congregate there, while at the same time he recognized an emerging trend which saw artists returning to their origins. This decentralization, of which he was a part, was, according to him, "bound to result in a wider interest in creative endeavor. This interest in time will result too in a more vigorous American art, for nothing stimulates the artist more than an interested audience." Furthermore, he believed that an "interested audience" was also a well-educated one, so he appealed for more art instruction in local schools, and soon dedicated much of his own energy to teaching.

Hirsch's earliest teaching affiliation was with the Gibbes Art Gallery, where fellow instructors were William Halsey and Corrie McCallum. Halsey was a native Charlestonian and his circumstances and attitudes mirrored Hirsch's. Halsey elected to pursue his art education elsewhere, over the objection of his mentor Verner. He felt that his birthplace had little to offer, so he went to the Museum School in Boston. Like Hirsch, Halsey was absent from Charleston for most of the period 1932 to 1944/1945. When his New York dealer invited Halsey to settle there, he demurred, "I was born in Charleston and came back here because I felt strongly that there were too many artists in a few areas and too few artists in small cities and towns and that I could be vastly more useful in my native state than any place else."[2] This sentiment exactly parallels Hirsch's statement to the cadets about "decentralization."

Hirsch, Halsey, and McCallum taught side by side at the Gibbes Art Gallery, though not without friction. They all needed teaching to supplement their incomes from the sale of art, which in conservative Charleston was always a struggle. The city had virtually no commercial galleries whose sole purpose was to promote and display contemporary art. To address this vacuum all three became active in the Guild of South Carolina Artists, a statewide membership organization established in 1952 to give artists exposure through annual circulating exhibitions. After about eight years at the Gibbes, a brouhaha arose concerning the city's financial support of the institution. The upshot of the dispute was the dissolution of the school. Cut off from their livelihood, the three founded the Charleston Art School. Hirsch conducted his classes in his studio on Exchange Street while around the corner Halsey and McCallum taught in a dependency structure behind a State Street property they rented. The collaboration continued for over ten years. Hirsch continued to teach afterward in his studio at 2 Queen Street, once an antebellum warehouse.

In addition to teaching, Hirsch pursued his own work. Perhaps inspired by his family situation—Hirsch and his wife lived with her family—he turned to Old Testament subjects, which he carved out of various kinds of wood. Like many sculptors of his generation, he admired the work of both Michelangelo and Auguste Rodin, who were known for their carving abilities. Believing that the figure was embedded in the marble or wood, they strove to release it, working intuitively with the inherent veins and cracks. Frequently the figure is not fully developed, but seems to be emerging from the medium.

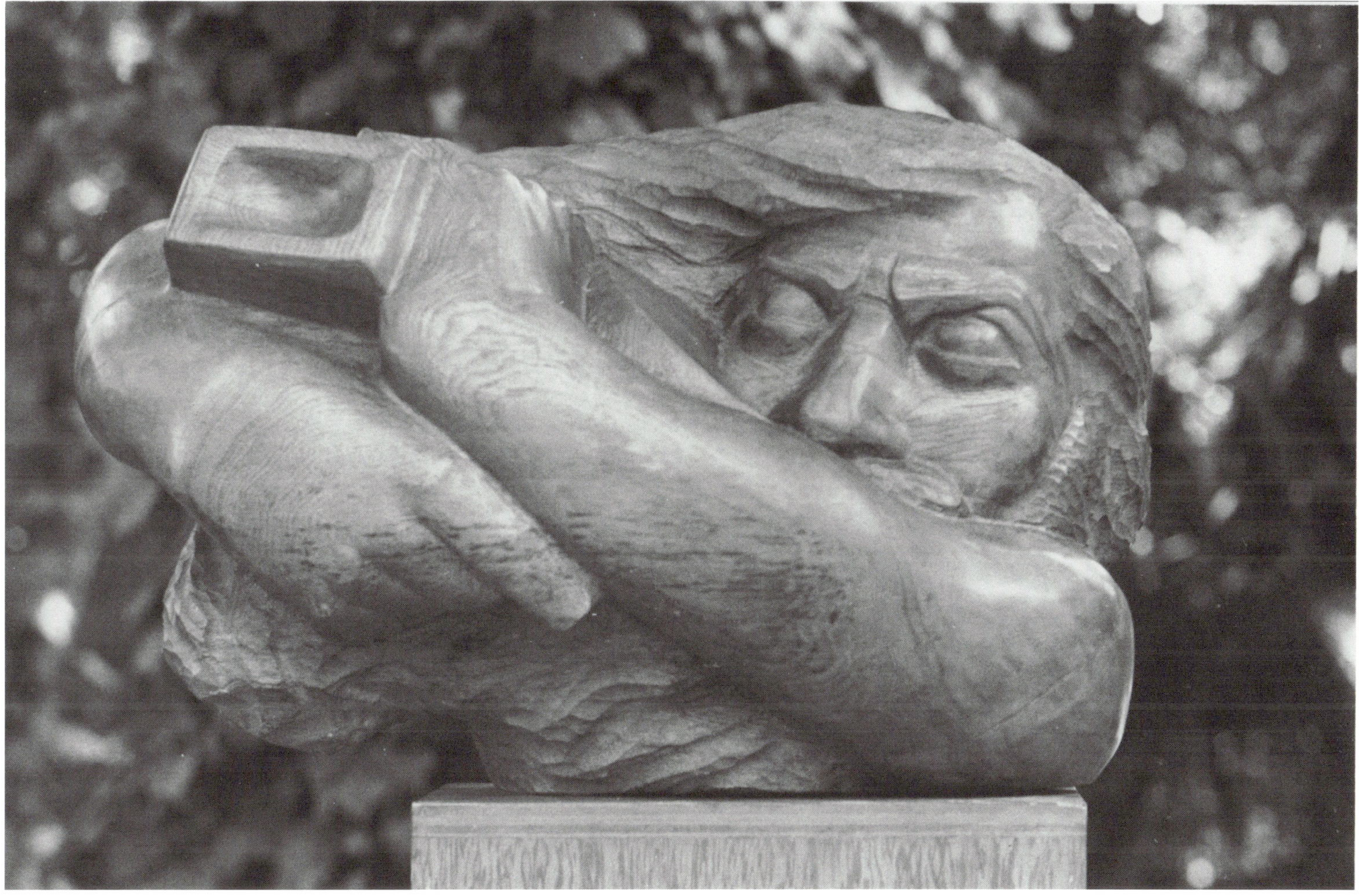

Fig. 6. Willard Hirsch, *Joshua at Jericho*, 1950. Red oak, 23 in. tall, Gibbes Museum of Art, Charleston, S.C. Photo by Louis Schwartz.

In emulation of these masters, Hirsch was adventuresome in the woods he selected. In *The Boy Joseph (see Figure 1)* and *David the Psalmist,* the outer and lighter sapwood furnishes the clothing and the expressive dark inner core becomes the tone of flesh. *Joshua at Jericho (Figure 6)* was carved from a large, bark-covered green log of red oak and the final product is suggestive of great physical and spiritual strength. *Elijah Fed by the Ravens (Figure 7)*, in the collection of the Greenville County Museum of Art, was carved from live oak, an especially hard wood, and its curling, interlocking grain effectively merges with the feathers of the ravens and the prophet's whiskers. Unlike most of the wooden pieces, which are closed and compact, *Jacob's Dream*, in the collection of the Columbia Museum of Art, and carved from sycamore, has openings between the angels who hover over the sleeping prophet. The result is more carefree and lyrical, and seems to reflect Hirsch's mood at the time; he has explained that the angels resemble his future wife, whom he was courting during this period.

Some of the Old Testament figures are conceived more thoroughly as three-dimensional compositions than others. *Joshua at Jericho* and *Elijah Fed by the Ravens* have single viewpoints, while *David the Psalmist* has a

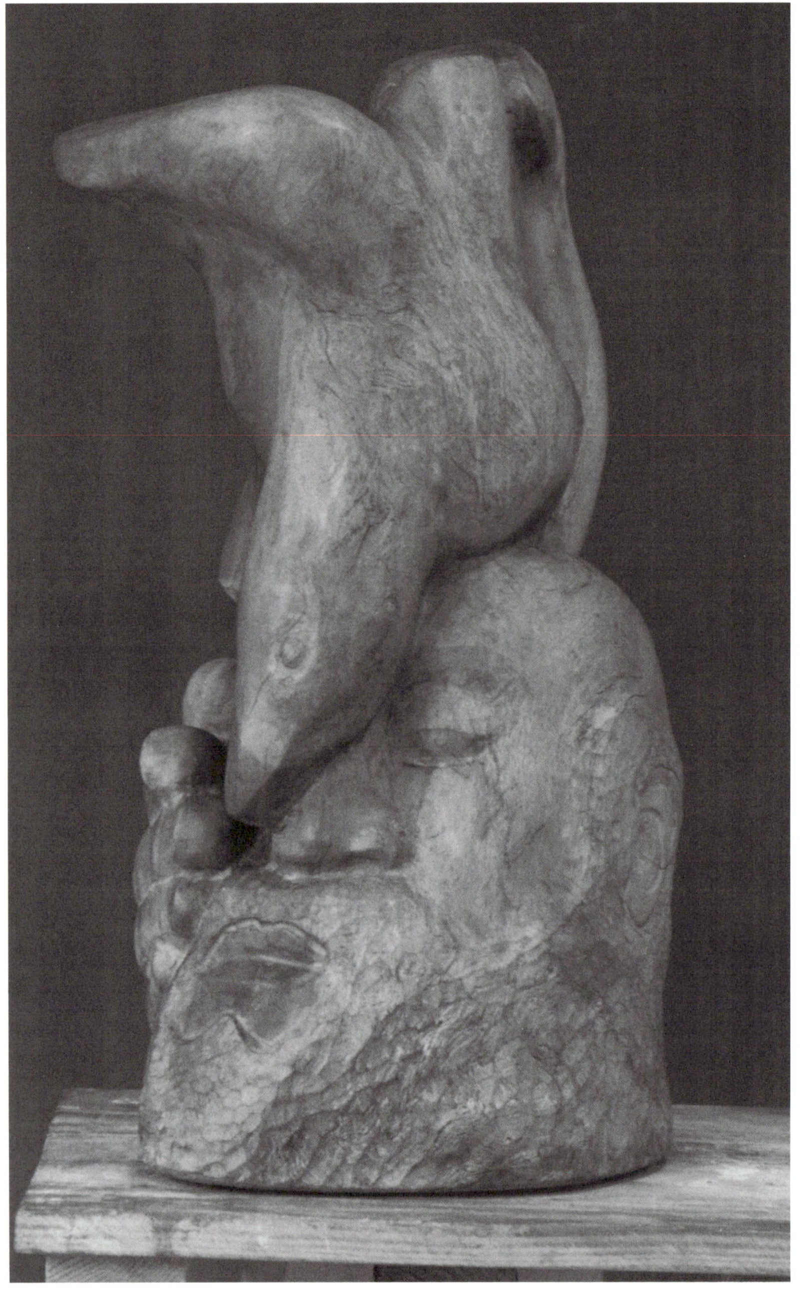

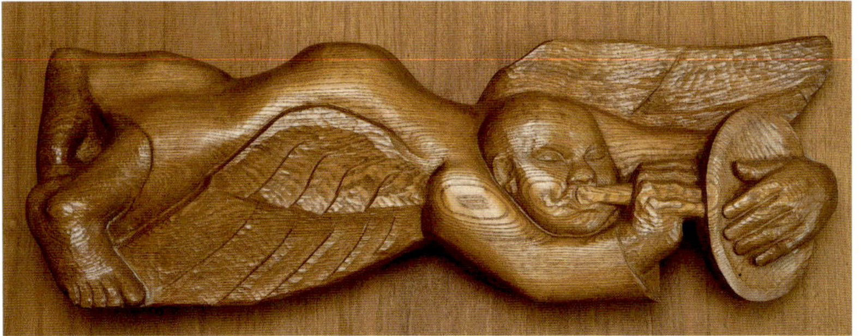

spiral format, which encourages the viewer to look at it from many sides. Another sculpture, *Gabriel with the Hot Trumpet (Figure 8)*—the subject inspired by a Negro spiritual—was created as a relief. Gabriel lies on his stomach and extends his body into a long, low profile. Blocky shapes of wings, head, buttocks, and hands are unified by the consistent horizontal wood grains, and are complemented by the natural patterns of the wood.

In 1970 Jack Morris, director of the Greenville County Museum of Art, compiled *Contemporary Artists of South Carolina* as part of the state's Tricentennial celebration. Of Hirsch's Old Testament sculptures, Morris wrote: "The success of these earlier works (1947–1948) is deeply rooted in the sense of rhythm and balance which is almost a by-product of the traditional sculptural concept based on the containment of forms within a block of material. In these works one is not only aware of the emotional tensions communicated by distortion of natural form and proportion but also of the physical intensity between artist and material. Each piece in the series evolves as a powerful visual statement not because of its literal representation, but in spite of it."[3]

Already, these early Charleston works reflect a consistent talent that persisted throughout Hirsch's career: sensitivity to his materials. Realizing that woodcarving was time-consuming, Hirsch turned to other avenues for the representation of Biblical subjects. For a Wheeling, West Virginia, synagogue he created two metal screens depicting the ascending and descending angels from Jacob's dream. (See *Figure 30*) Through the dull metallic surface of the angels, their welded and gilded edges, and their angular shapes

Fig. 7. Willard Hirsch, *Elijah Fed by the Ravens*, 1948-49. Live oak, 23 in. tall, Greenville County Museum of Art, Greenville, S.C. Photo by Louis Schwartz.

Fig. 8. Willard Hirsch, *Gabriel with the Hot Trumpet*, 1946. Ash, 36 in. long, Jack and Florence Kurtz collection. Photo by Douglas M. Pinkerton.

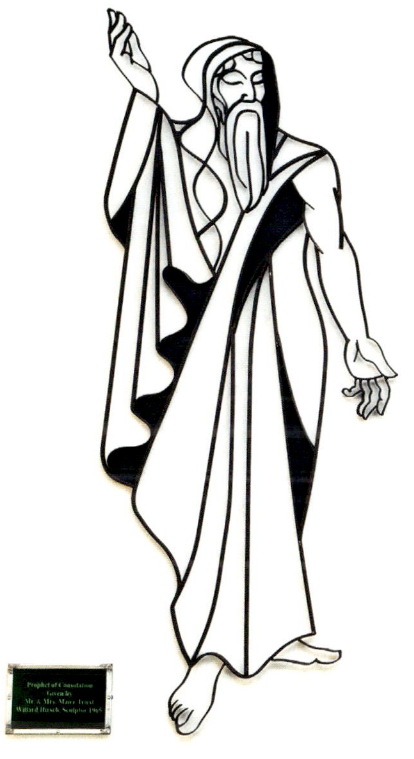

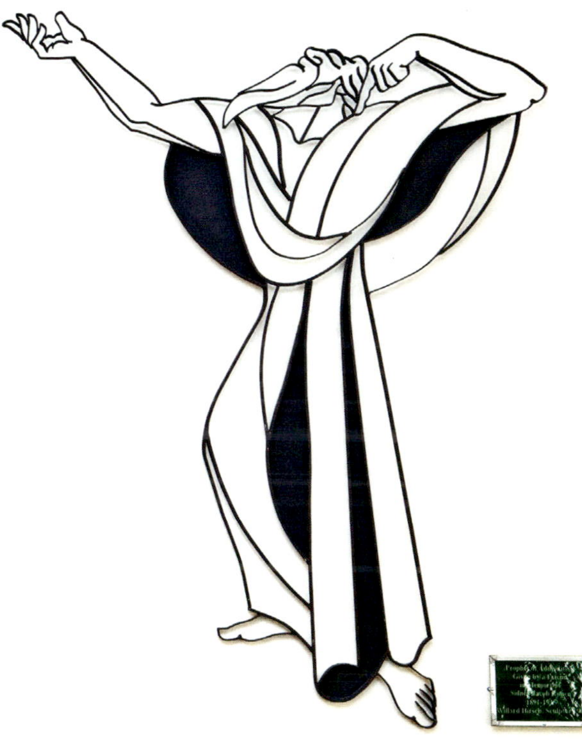

Fig. 9. (far left) Willard Hirsch, *The Prophet of Admonition*, 1965. Steel, 5 ¼ ft. tall, Kahol Kadosh Beth Elohim Synagogue, Charleston, S.C. Photo by Douglas M. Pinkerton.

Fig. 10. (left) Willard Hirsch, *The Prophet of Consolation*, 1965. Steel, 5 ¼ ft. tall, Kahol Kadosh Beth Elohim Synagogue, Charleston, S.C. Photo by Douglas M. Pinkerton.

Fig. 11. (below left) Willard Hirsch, *Jonah*, 1963. Steel and brass, 52 in. tall, Emanu-El Synagogue, Charleston, S.C. Photo by Douglas M. Pinkerton.

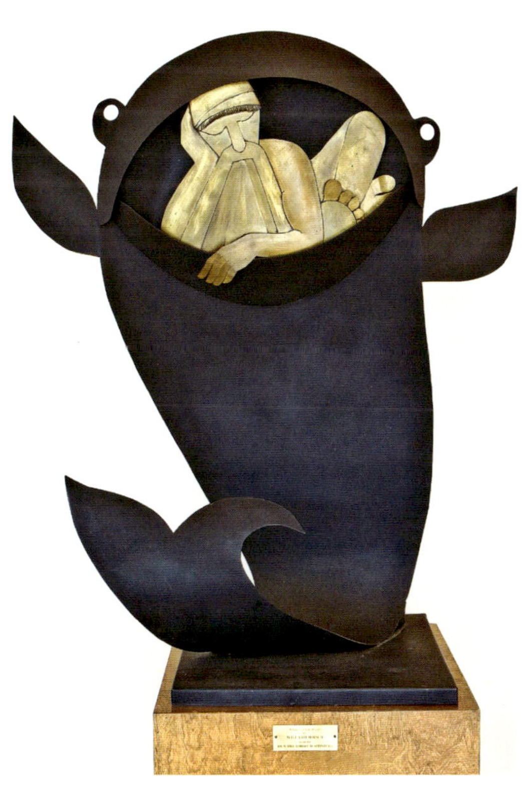

coupled with the openings of the screens themselves, Hirsch accomplished the feeling of a vertical, uplifting movement—most appropriate for panels flanking the ark and pulpit of a synagogue. For the social hall of Charleston's Kahal Kadosh Beth Elohim, Hirsch fashioned two allegorical figures out of thin bands of wrought iron, which define their outlines and their garments. The simple reduction to linear silhouettes is reminiscent of the drawings and paintings of the French modernist Henri Matisse, whereas the emphatic and expressive gestures of *The Prophet of Consolation* and *The Prophet of Admonition (Figures 9* and *10)* recall Donatello's stern prophet statues for the Campanile in Florence. In a more playful vein, the steel and brass *Jonah,* more than four feet tall, shows the prophet curled up inside the jaws of an imposing whale that appears to balance on his tail. *(Figure 11)* All three of these metal sculptures rely heavily on bold shapes

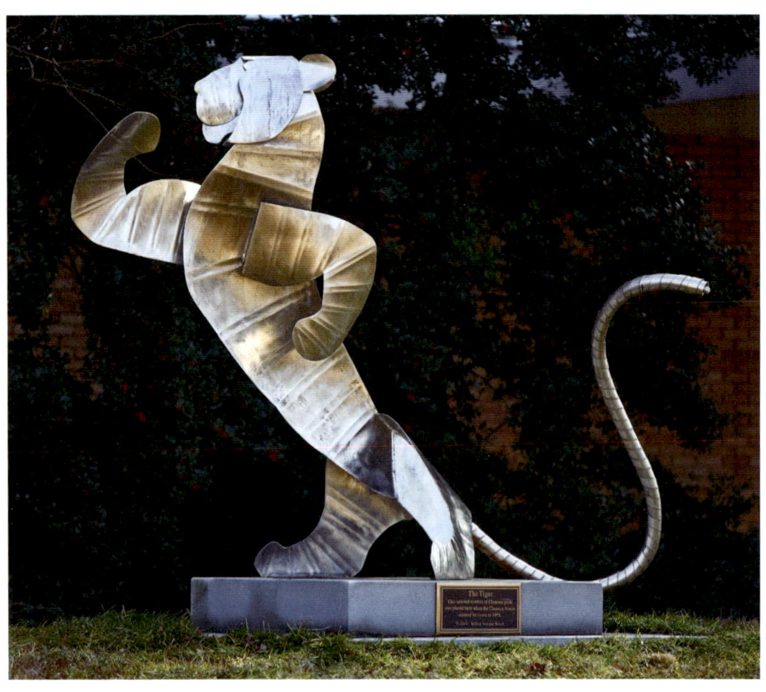

Fig. 12. Willard Hirsch, *The Clemson Tiger*, 1949. Stainless steel, 7 ft. tall, Clemson University, Clemson, S.C. Photo by Douglas M. Pinkerton.

and outlined forms, qualities that are made easier in metal than in wood.

Perhaps Hirsch's best-known metal commission was Clemson University's mascot. *The Clemson Tiger (Figure 12)*, originally enhanced by his position over a reflecting pool, was cleverly conceived and the result is an engaging monument. The strong upward diagonal of its body is extended by its upraised right paw—perhaps a gesture of athletic victory?—and balanced by the sprightly S-curve of its long tail. In its emphasis on silhouette and its simplification, *The Tiger* verges on caricature. Sixty years after Hirsch created this beloved symbol, an inscription describes it as a "spirited example of Clemson pride" that "was placed here when Clemson House opened its doors in 1951."

Metal was an ideal material for outdoor sculptures. In a commission dating to 1960 for the Charleston County Public Library on King Street and Marion Square, Hirsch clustered together seven figures in the act of reading in what he called a "steel drawing." *(Figure 13)* The shiny steel with its high sheen complemented the modernistic building. At the top a man in glasses holds a large volume, and a man and woman below in profile intently focus on their books. In the middle, seen from behind, is someone reading a newspaper, and underneath him a pair of children concentrate on their volumes. Curves of bodies counterbalance the angular shapes of the books, creating a harmonious whole that celebrates the art of reading. For the children's room, Hirsch selected characters from *Alice in Wonderland* to enliven the entrance, to welcome young readers to the

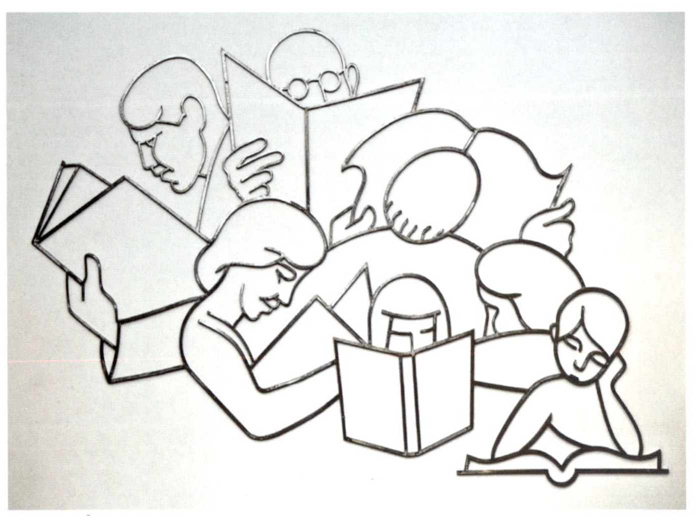

Fig. 13. Willard Hirsch, *Readers*, 1961. Stainless steel, 6 ft. 4 in. wide X 4 ft. 8 in. tall, Charleston County Public Library, Charleston, S.C. Photo by Douglas M. Pinkerton.

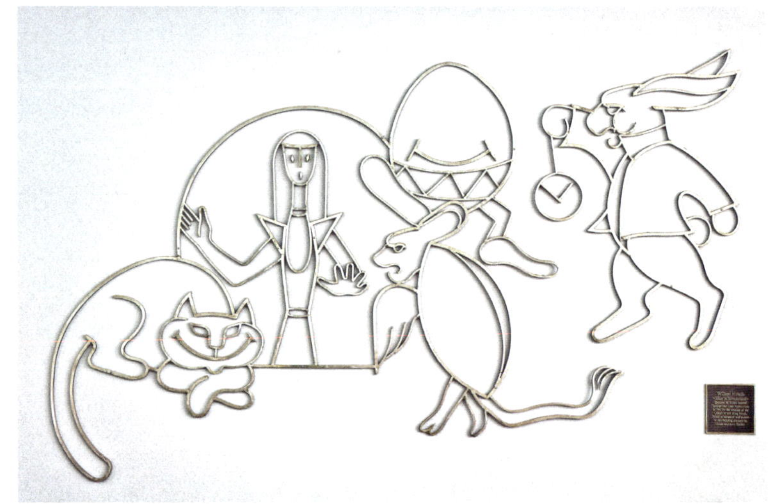

Fig. 14. Willard Hirsch, *Alice in Wonderland*, 1961. Stainless steel, 7 ft. wide X 3 ½ ft. tall, Charleston County Public Library, Charleston, S.C. Photo by Douglas M. Pinkerton.

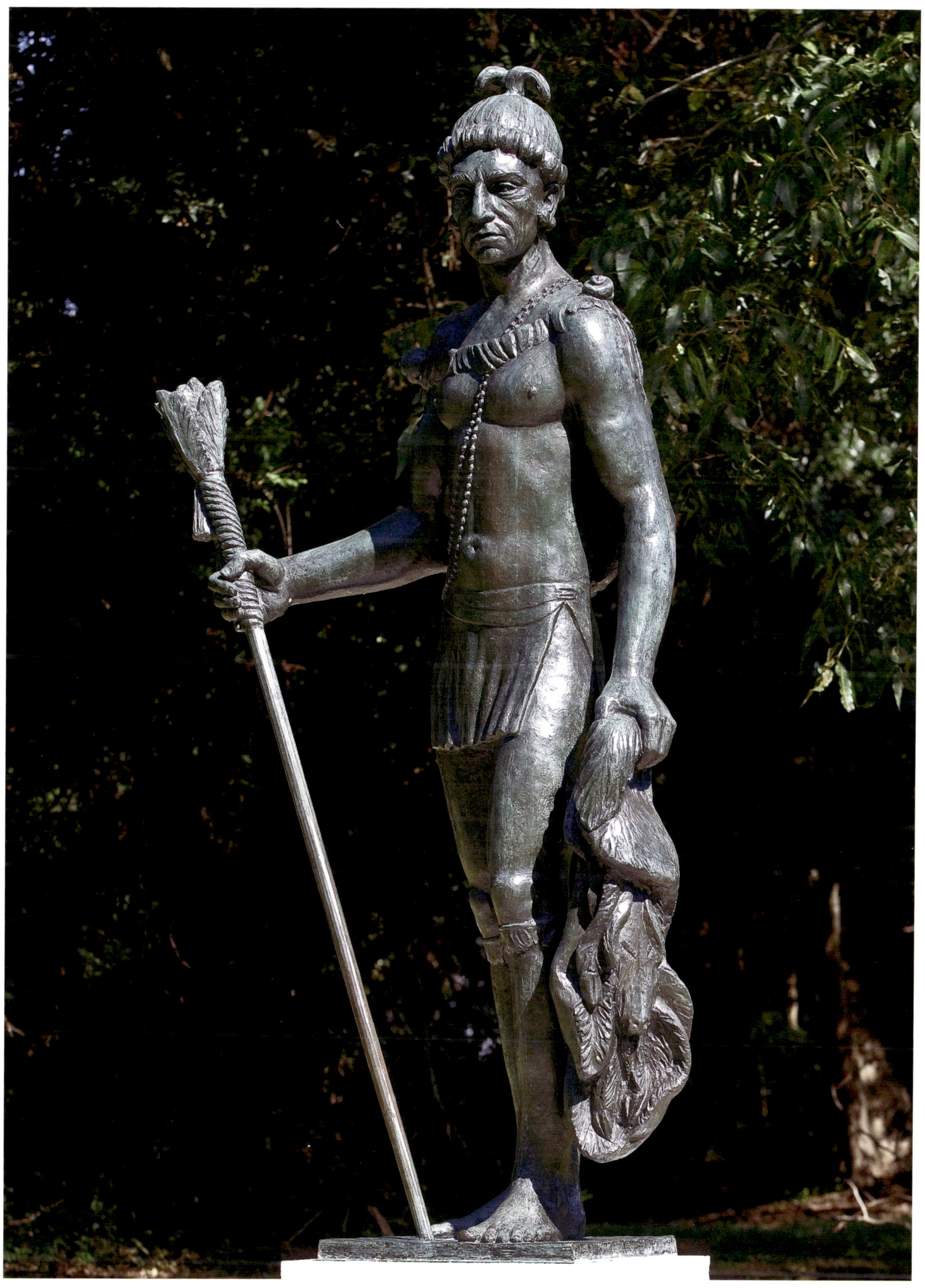

Fig. 15. Willard Hirsch, *Cassique of Kiawah*, 1971-72. Bronze, 8½ ft. tall, Charles Towne Landing, Charleston, S.C. Photo by Douglas M. Pinkerton.

world of Alice, Humpty Dumpty, and the Cheshire Cat. *(Figure 14)* When the library moved to new quarters, the much-loved artworks were transferred and they continue to convey their message of knowledge and community to younger generations.

Obtaining commissions for public buildings was of critical importance to Hirsch, not only because of the compensation he received, but also because of the satisfaction he derived from reaching "interested audiences." An artist who came of age during the 1930s, when New Deal programs brought art to the people in the form of paintings and sculptures designed for post offices and courthouses, Hirsch believed in the enriching benefits of art. As he told the Citadel cadets, "sculpture is a vital living art in America. ... A work of art is conceived and produced to bring to the beholder something of the vision of the artist. Respect it, yes, but by all means enjoy it."[4]

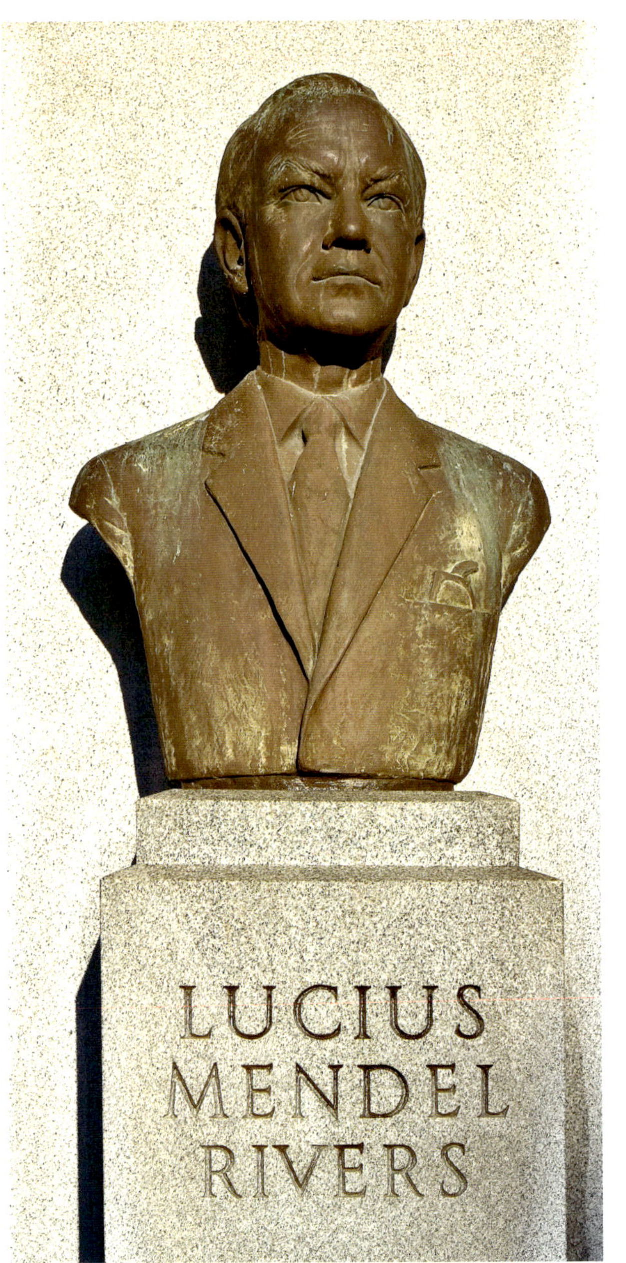

Fig. 16. Willard Hirsch, *Lucius Mendel Rivers*, 1971. Bronze, 30½ in. tall, Charleston County Office Building, Charleston, S.C. Photo by Douglas M. Pinkerton.

One commission that has brought Hirsch lasting recognition, is the *Cassique of Kiawah*, for Charles Towne Landing. *(Figure 15)* Devised as part of the state's Tricentennial in 1970, the historic site was developed to commemorate the landing and early settlement of Europeans in South Carolina. A cassique or cacique is a native prince, and in his 1859 fictional history of early Charleston, novelist William Gilmore Simms described one such Native American: "He at the stern [of a canoe] is evidently a chief. He wears a sort of coronal of feathers, and a gay crimson coat, hunting-shirt fashion, with yellow fringes, evidently the manufacture of the white man. There is a belt across his shoulders, from which hangs the tomahawk; another about his waist, which secures his knife; his right hand grasps bow and arrows, though the former remains unbent, and the latter lie bundled together innocuous in their rattlesnake quiver."[5] While Hirsch's interpretation differs from Simms's description, the larger-than-life sculpture radiates power and dignity. His heroic demeanor, well-developed musculature, and focused gaze are reminiscent of Michelangelo's *David*, which Hirsch greatly admired, even though he never saw it in person. But unlike its completely nude Renaissance predecessor, the *Cassique of Kiawah* is embellished and enlivened by many fine details: the beads and strap across his shoulders; the crown of feathers; the staff or spear in his right hand, and the animal skin in his left. Hirsch worked out all of these details in his half-size clay model, which was enlarged and transformed into bronze at the foundry.

The *Cassique of Kiawah* was unique in Hirsch's oeuvre; he was never given the opportunity to develop another similar figure. This kind of public monument—to be displayed out of doors—was what he had been trained to do during his student days in New York, and was the type of commission that came to many of his northern colleagues. Here, finally, was a major sculpture—measuring eight-and-a-half feet in height—in which Hirsch got to celebrate the land of his birth.

Portraiture—a longstanding and venerable tradition in Charleston—helped to sustain Hirsch and supplement income gained from other commissions and teaching. He worked in a variety of materials and formats, including bronze and terra-cotta reliefs and busts. The opportunity to work on commemorative pieces was attractive to Hirsch, who hoped they would bring recognition and further work. Perhaps his most visible portrait is that of U.S. Congressman Mendel Rivers which is enshrined on a pedestal, surrounded by severe stone walls inscribed with a lofty tribute, "Patriot and statesman. … He spoke for his neighbors and strove to keep his country strong." *(Figure 16)* In keeping with its setting near the Charleston County Office Building, the image is reserved, if not severe. In contrast, Hirsch's portrayal in bronze relief of noted Charleston architect and preservationist Albert Simons for the fine arts building at the College of Charleston is more endearing, perhaps because sculptor and architect shared the same Beaux Arts training and mutual respect. *(Figure 17)* No longer a young man, Simons is shown in a characteristic expression, a slight smile on his lips, with his oversize glasses slid halfway down his nose. Underneath, the inscription bears a message close to Hirsch's own raison d'être: "In appreciation for years of dedication to the fine arts."

Fig. 17. Willard Hirsch, *Albert Simons*, 1978. Bronze, 24½ in. tall, Albert Simons Fine Arts Building, College of Charleston, Charleston, S.C. Photo by Douglas M. Pinkerton.

Hirsch developed a sub-specialty: terra-cotta portrait heads. *(Figures 18 and 19)* Following the tradition of Roman portraits, he recorded the distinctive features of each individual. Like his ancient predecessors, he either left the eyes blank or incised a circle to designate the iris. Rarely does the sitter smile, or wear any article of clothing—with one notable exception, his daughter Jane, who wore her tennis hat. Whereas wrinkles and rumpled clothes distinguish

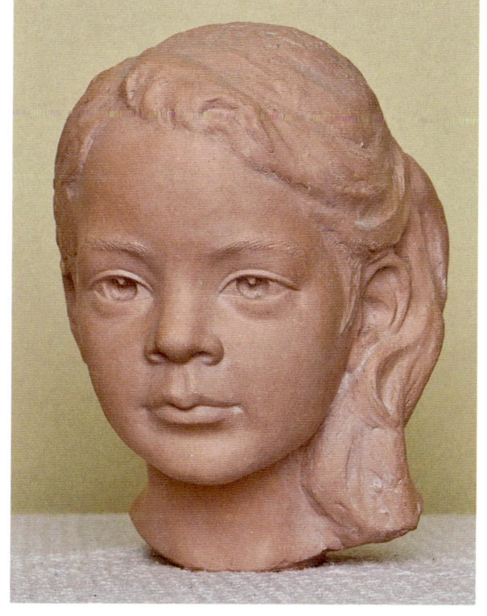

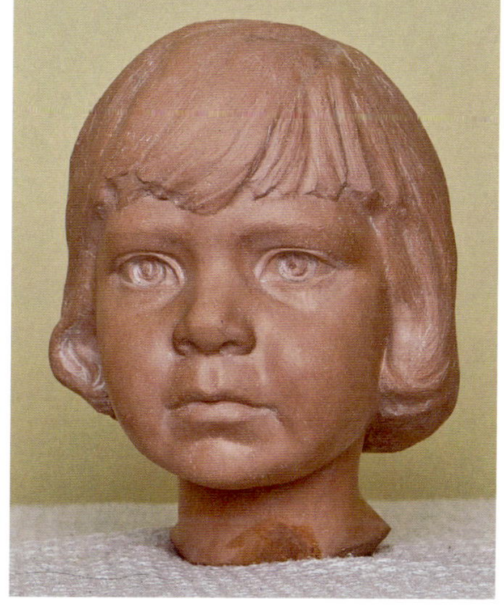

Fig. 18. (far left)Willard Hirsch, *Child's head*, n.d. Terra-cotta, 9½ in. tall, private collection. Photo by Douglas M. Pinkerton.

Fig. 19. (left) Willard Hirsch, *Child's head*, n.d. Terra-cotta, 8 ¾ in. tall, private collection. Photo by Douglas M. Pinkerton.

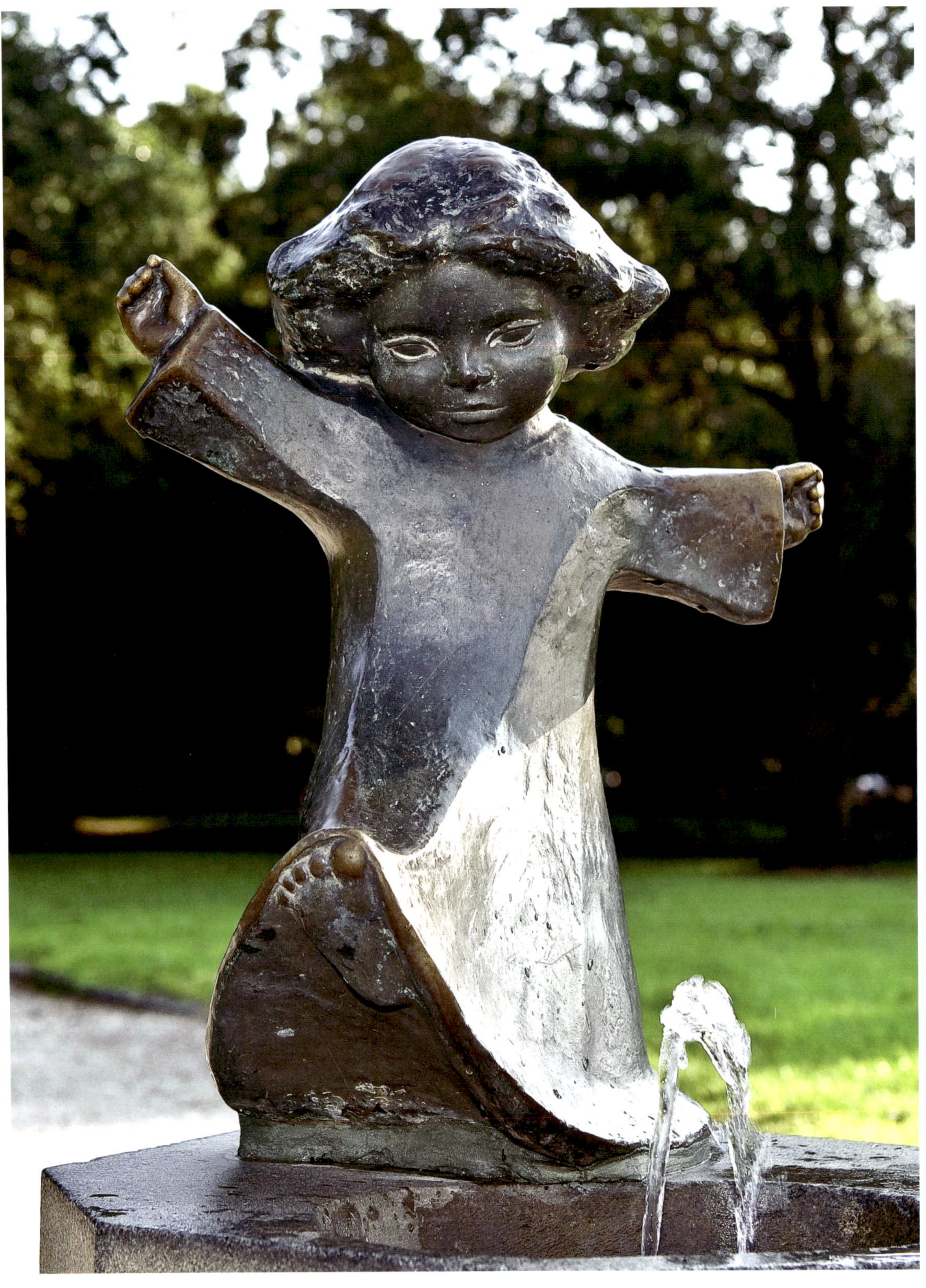

Fig. 20. Willard Hirsch, *Little Dancer*, 1950s. Bronze, 22 in. tall, White Point Garden, Charleston, S.C. Photo by Douglas M. Pinkerton.

elder citizens like Simons, Hirsch's children are fresh and unmarked by emotions. The warm flesh-like tone of the terra-cotta, however, serves to soften the likenesses. In his portraits of women the hairdo often stands out, as seen in his portrayals of his wife and the artist Anne Worsham Richardson. (See *Figure 58*)

The majority of the terra-cotta busts, or heads, were of women and children, which coincided nicely with the independent work he was doing. Perhaps Hirsch's best-known and most-beloved figure in this category is the *Little Dancer (Figure 20),* the depiction of a delightfully spirited young girl who kicks up her right foot and full skirt and raises her arms in apparent glee. While more than one *Little Dancer* exists, the most familiar is at White Point Garden in Charleston, where many local citizens and tourists have been refreshed by her sense of joy. Here, she is positioned above a water fountain, giving the illusion that she is dancing or wading in a spring.

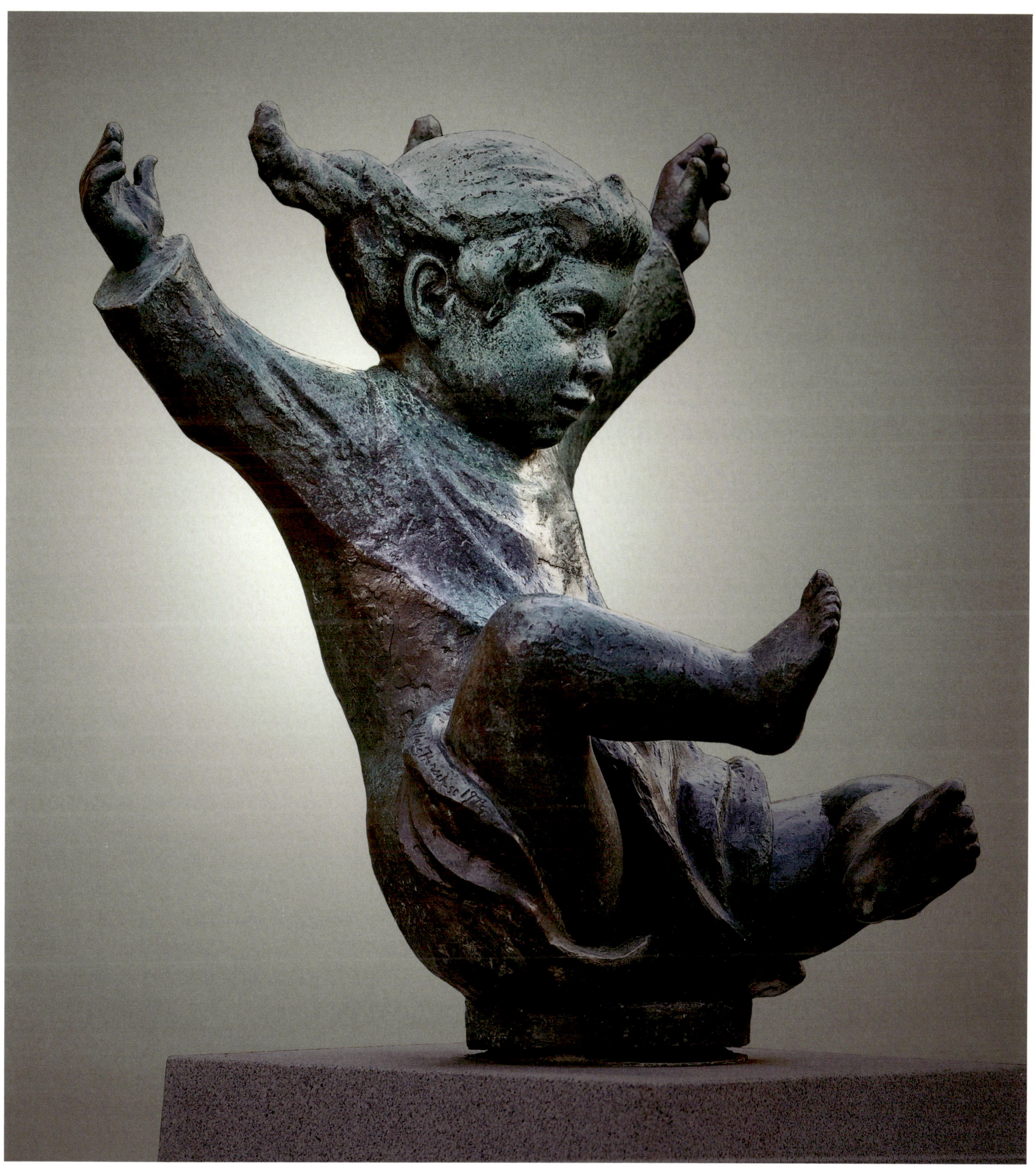

Fig. 21. Willard Hirsch, *Falling Angel,* 1980. Bronze, 22 in. tall, Gibbes Museum of Art, Charleston, S.C. Photo by Douglas M. Pinkerton.

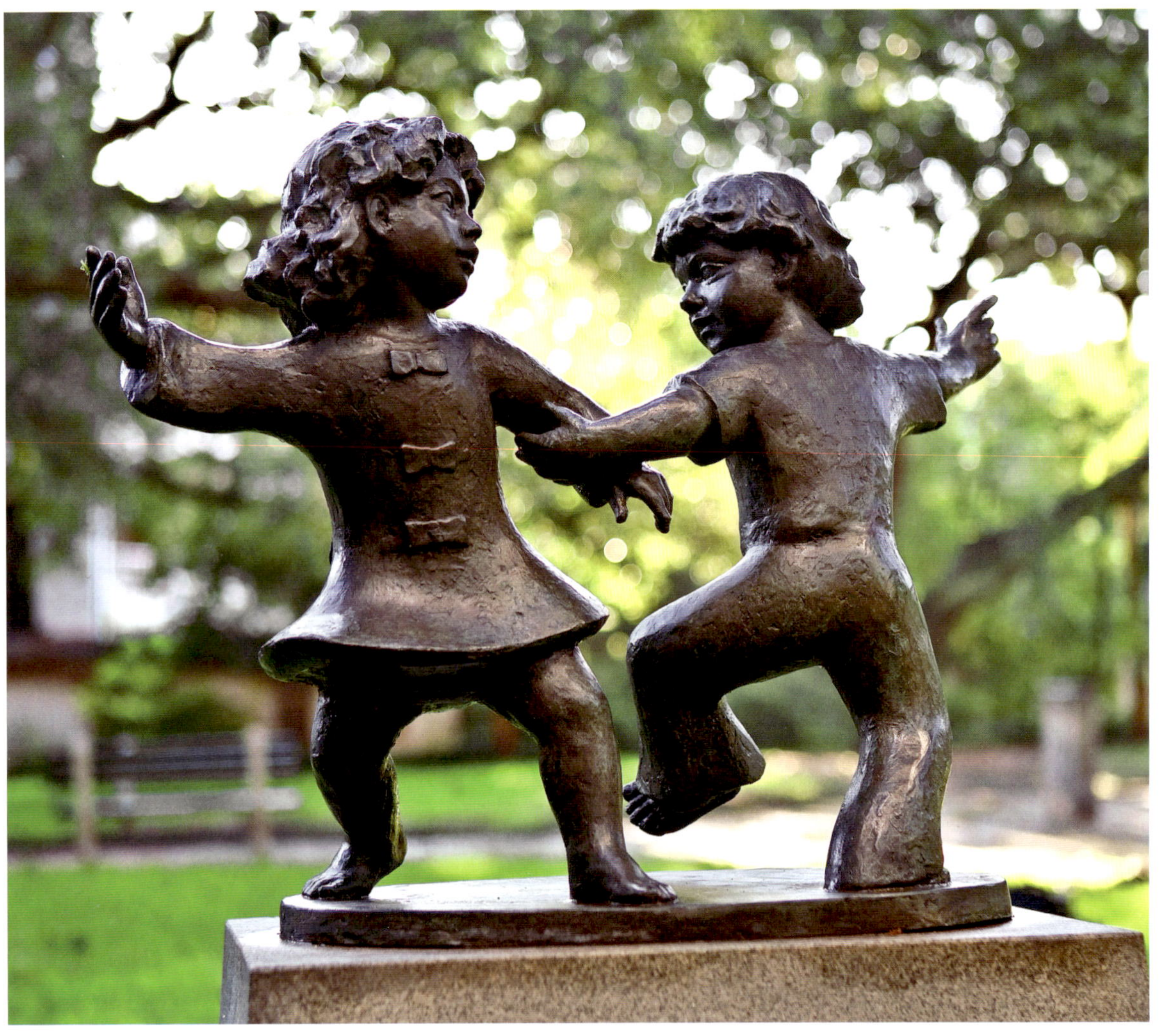

Fig. 22. Willard Hirsch, *Do-Si-Do*, 1981. Bronze, 22 in. tall, Washington Square Park, Charleston, S.C. Photo by Douglas M. Pinkerton.

The popularity of the *Little Dancer* bore fruit in several versions, including miniatures, which Hirsch produced in limited editions. In addition, a virtual family of siblings was born: the *Falling Angel* and the *Do-Si-Do*. Like her sister, the young girl in *Falling Angel (Figure 21)* expresses carefree abandon, as she lands on her posterior with her arms upraised and her pigtails flying. In contrast to the blocky garment of the *Little Dancer*, the angel's drape clings across her torso and is pulled up revealing her pudgy legs. Appropriately, *Falling Angel* was selected as a tribute to her maker by a group of his admirers, and was installed until recently in front of the Gibbes Art Gallery School on Queen Street, where he had taught for so many years. In the *Do-Si-Do (Figure 22),* Hirsch used similarly proportioned children, and intertwined them in an arrangement that succeeds from any angle. Again, gaiety is the theme, as the figures artfully complement one another and revolve around in the act of dancing. Their situation in a gracious and leafy corner of Washington Square Park near the Fireproof Building gives them a public venue as they pay tribute to Marguerite Valk, a noted Charleston preservationist.

While these youthful figures testify to the sculptor's joie de vivre, none speaks more lovingly of this spirit than his *Joy of Motherhood (Figure 23).* Once the centerpiece in the lobby of a savings and loan institution, a posthumous cast now graces a spot near a reflecting pool at Brookgreen Gardens. The composition is intricately balanced, with the graceful and attenuated limbs of the mother offset by her airborne ponytail. She carefully steadies her baby on her knee, and together they exchange glances that speak of the incredible bond between a mother and her child. It is only appropriate that Willard Hirsch's *Joy of Motherhood* is

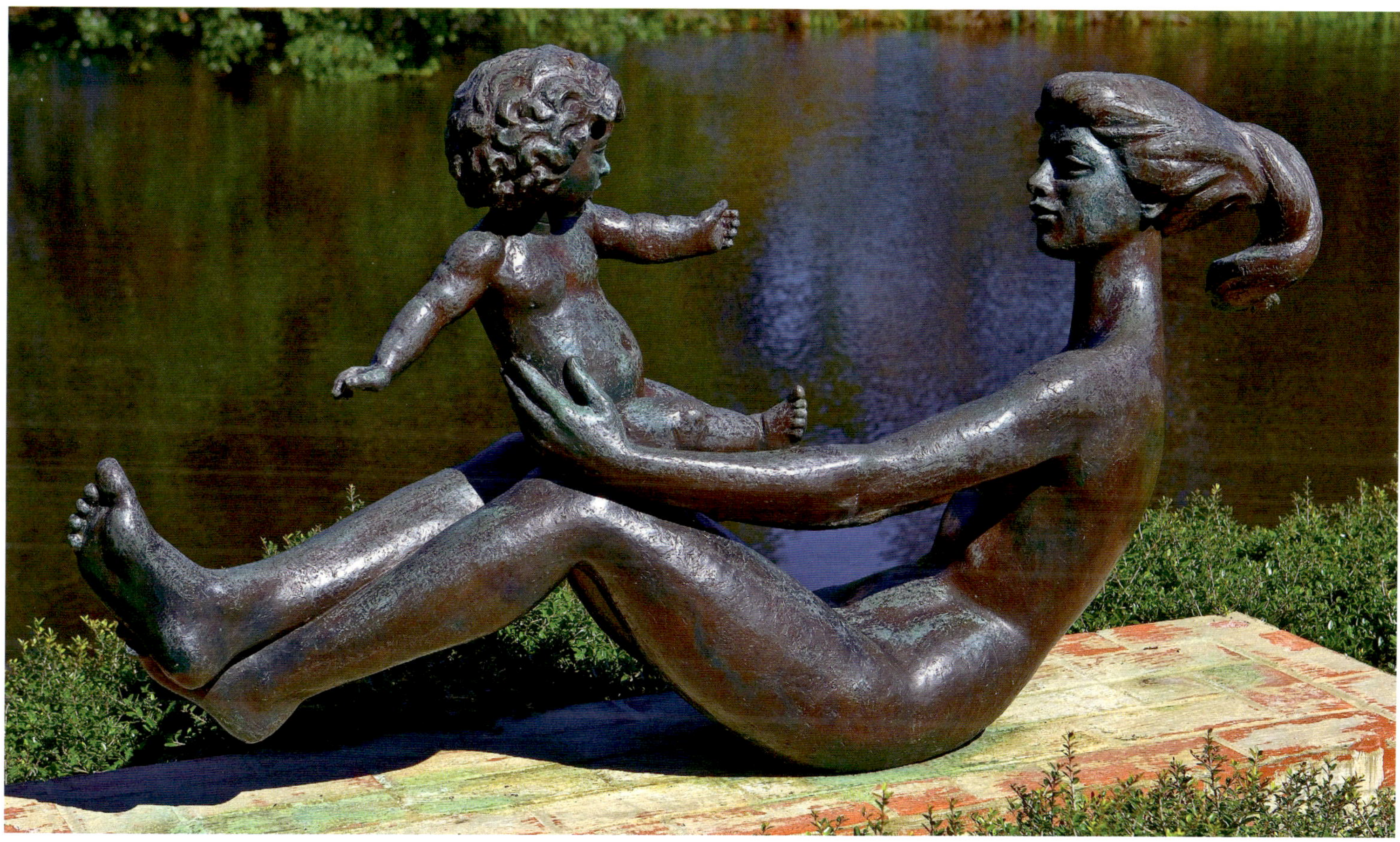

Fig. 23. Willard Hirsch, *Joy of Motherhood*, 1970. Bronze, 29½ in. tall X 56 in. wide X 15 in. deep. Brookgreen Gardens, Murrells Inlet, S.C. Photo by Douglas M. Pinkerton.

enshrined at Brookgreen Gardens, the outdoor home of the most extensive collection of figurative sculpture in this country. One of only a handful of pieces by South Carolina artists there, *Joy of Motherhood* joins sculptures by his teachers and colleagues, and is a fitting tribute to the man who decided to return home and make his way as Charleston's premier sculptor of the twentieth century.

Martha R. Severens is a graduate of Wells College, Aurora, N.Y., and earned a master's degree from the Johns Hopkins University. She served as curator of collections at the Gibbes Museum of Art, 1976–1987, and organized a retrospective of Willard Hirsch's work in 1979. For five years she worked at the Portland (Maine) Museum of Art, and in 1992 returned to South Carolina to be curator at the Greenville County Museum of Art. She retired in April 2010.

---

[1] Hirsch, lecture to Citadel cadets, February 26, 1945, Willard Hirsch papers at the Marlene & Nathan Addlestone Library of the College of Charleston. Subsequent quotations are from this lecture.

[2] Halsey, application to the John Simon Guggenheim Foundation, October 1952, quoted in Jack A. Morris, Jr., *William M. Halsey: Retrospective* (Greenville, S.C.: Greenville County Museum of Art, 1972), 29.

[3] Jack A. Morris, *Contemporary Artists of South Carolina* (Greenville, S.C.: Greenville County Museum of Art, 1970), 107.

[4] William Gilmore Simms, *The Cassique of Kiawah: A Colonial Romance* (New York: Redfield, 1859), 16-17.

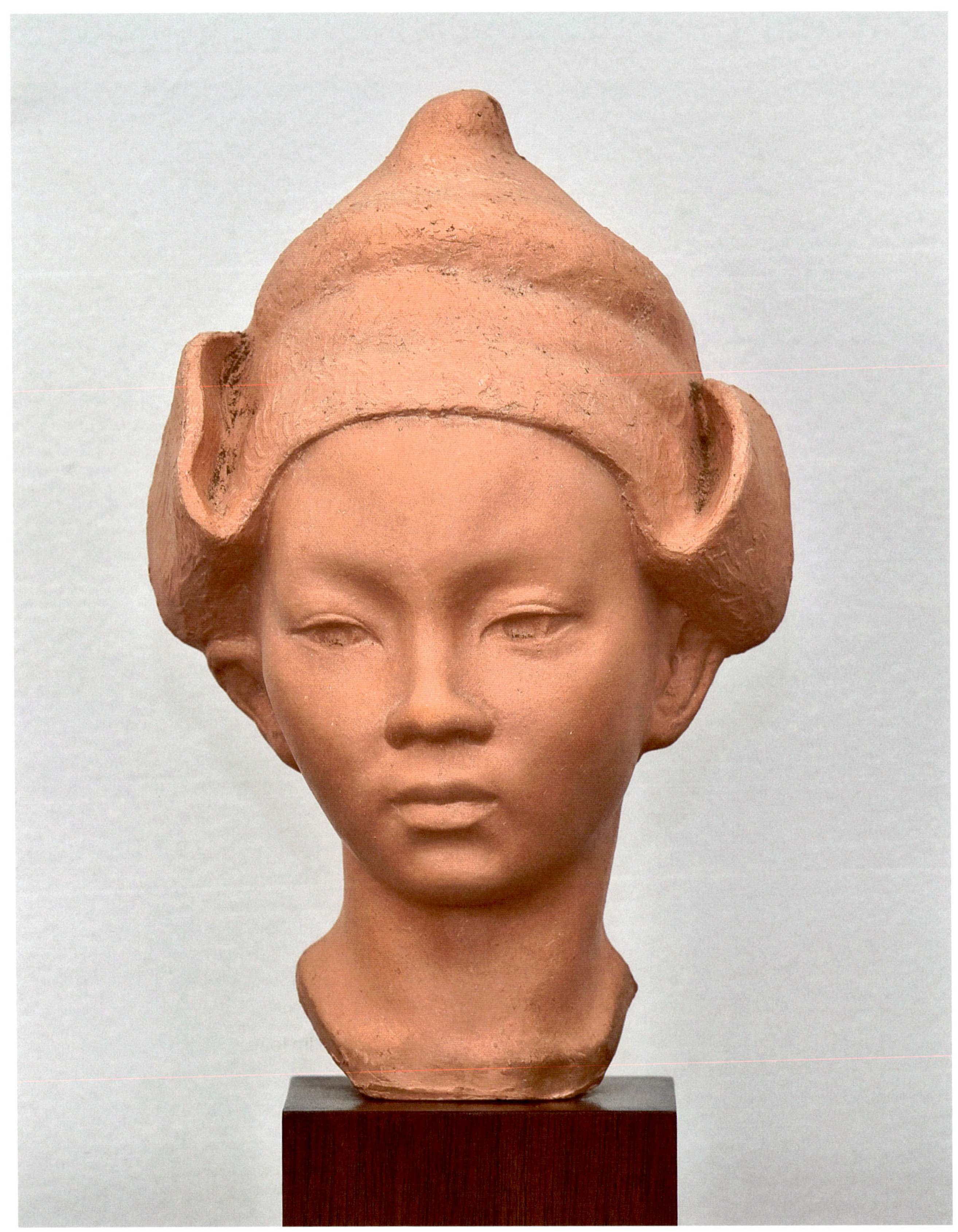

Fig. 25. Willard Hirsch, *Chinese Boy,* late 1930s. Terra-cotta, 9¾ in. tall X 9 in. wide, private collection. Photo by Douglas M. Pinkerton.

Laissez-faire Artist and Southern Gentleman

Mordenai Raisin Hirsch

The Hirsches were long-time members of Kahol Kadosh Beth Elohim, the congregation of my father, Rabbi Jacob Raisin, so in a way we always knew each other. A. A. Hirsch and Miriam Newman Hirsch had four children: Willard, Roslyn, Marion, and Elizabeth. *(Figure 24)* I knew Roslyn as Miss Hirsch, one of our religious-school teachers. When I had an occasion to speak to Willard, it was "Mr. Hirsch," the proper way to address someone more than twelve years my senior.

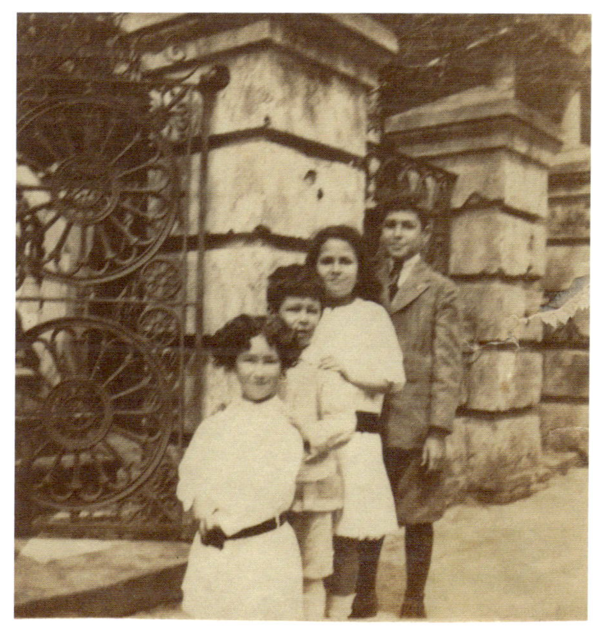

Fig. 24. The Hirsch siblings, front to back: Elizabeth, Marion, Roslyn, and Willard, 1917. Hirsch family colloction.

There was relatively little socializing between our families. After the untimely death of her husband at age forty-four, Mrs. Hirsch and the two girls moved north to be with her family in New York. Marion was sent to live with an uncle in Philadelphia, perhaps because of finances. I never knew him until my wedding.

Willard attended the College of Charleston until 1927, when his father died. Without having graduated, he went to work at what is now the Triest Insurance Agency to help support the family. He was about twenty-seven when his uncle in New York wrote that he had found a job for him, so he left to join the family up north. That job did not materialize.

Noting Willard's skill in molding animals from the wax dripping from the Sabbath candles as the family sat around the supper table, an aunt offered to pay his tuition for art classes. He applied to and was accepted at the National Academy of Design. The story is that his brother Marion convinced him to visit a well-known sculptor and professor at the National Academy, who told him that he needed to submit a piece of his work, which he didn't have. So, he sat his mother on a kitchen stool, sculpted her head, and "fired" it in her kitchen oven. The sculptor was impressed with this and helped him to get accepted. Willard also studied at the Beaux Arts Institute and then opened his own studio in New York City. He was able to continue his art education through scholarships and prizes that he won, such as for *Chinese Boy (Figure 25)*, his first piece to win a prize. He maintained a studio in New York for ten years, from 1932 to 1942.

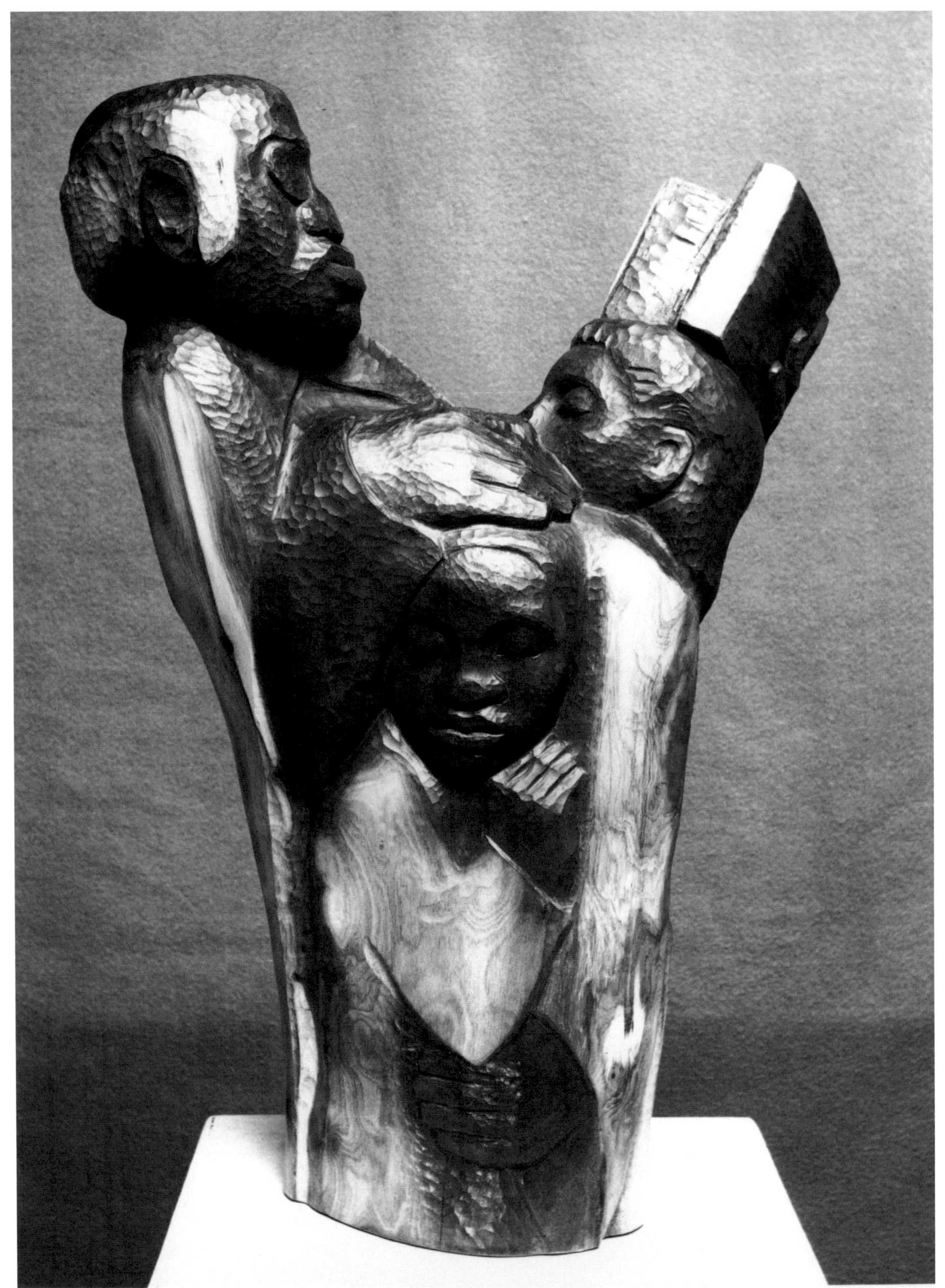

Fig. 26. Willard Hirsch, *God's Children*, 1948. Walnut, 32 in. tall, private collection. Photo by Louis Schwartz.

In 1942, at the age of thirty-seven (although with a severe hearing loss, which is thought to have resulted from a problem with his tonsils in his teenage years), he was drafted into the army. Willard was stationed at Fort Jackson in Columbia, South Carolina. When his commanding officer heard that he was "good with clay," he was assigned to design a baseball diamond. Later, when his talents became known, he spent many hours doing portrait busts of the commanding officers. In 1944 he was separated from the service and returned to Charleston, where he opened a studio on Exchange Street and began his thirty-five-year career as a sculptor in Charleston.

My memories of our courtship are scarce. Willard told me that he first noticed me as an adult in 1947, when he passed the synagogue building one Saturday morning and saw me on the portico. He even remembered that I wore a white eyelet piqué dress! He borrowed my family's car to take me out one evening, and on our return we sat in the car for hours talking.

One of my favorite memories is his offer to prepare supper for my family one night. His specialty was fish chowder. He made such a huge potful that we ate it for weeks!

We saw each other later in 1947, while I was finishing my master's degree at Columbia Teachers College in New York and Willard was visiting his mother there. I went to her apartment for dinner, and he walked me back to my dorm—all thirty blocks!

When our engagement was announced in the Charleston *News and Courier* on May 15, 1949, Willard was in Philadelphia for the opening of an exhibit at the Whitney Museum, where his woodcarving *God's Children* had been accepted for the show. *(Figure 26)* Willard's friends implied that he'd be difficult to live with, but I excused any so-called faults as being those of an artistic persona. He had a caustic sense of humor, which was difficult for me to accept. Some of it was lost on me, and some I found embarrassing. After all, I was the daughter of a rabbi *(Figure 27)* and was taught by my mother to be a "southern lady." I never felt completely at ease among his artist friends.

Fig. 27. Willard Hirsch, *Rabbi Jacob Raisin*, late 1940s, bas relief, 12½ in. tall X 9 in. wide, Hirsch family collection. Photo by Douglas M. Pinkerton.

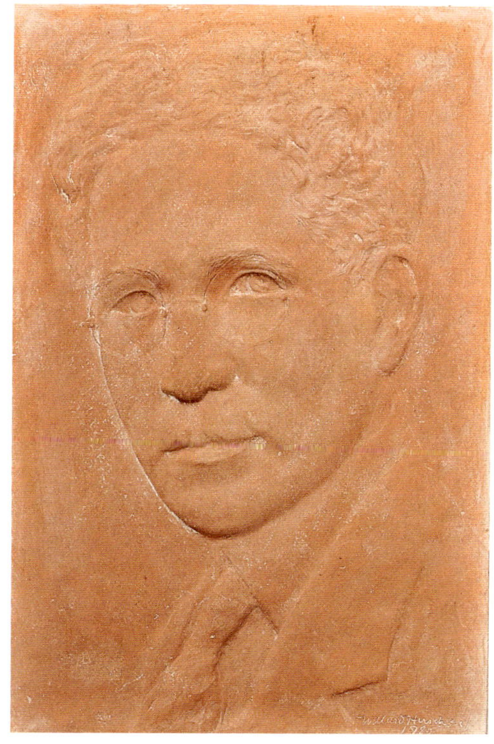

Willard was an interesting combination of laissez-faire artist and southern gentleman. Outside of his creative milieu, he was insensitive to the feelings of others. Once his sister Roslyn visited Charleston and arrived at the house to go out to lunch. She was wearing a pantsuit, which at the time was not accepted dress for ladies in Charleston. Willard refused to be seen with her.

He loved animals. His special hobby was keeping tropical fish, and he was considered a local authority on the subject. Willard had several large aquariums in his studio, many of which he had made, including saltwater tanks. The harbor pilots brought him fresh saltwater when they returned from moving container ships in or out of our port. If he had to be away, he would leave me written instructions as to what, when, and how to feed his "pets."

I like to think that Willard mellowed after our marriage. He loved his children and was very proud of them. When our son Jack was born, we decided to name him for his two grandfathers, Jacob and Alexander. Willard wrote his family that we were calling him Jalex—which produced a flurry of long-distance telephone calls (at that time a luxury) berating him for even thinking of such a thing. Willard often gave Jack his bottle, and we took a photo of them which he sent to family members with the caption, "Man is the only male mammal who can give milk." When Jack was a little boy, Willard would take him over to Colonial Lake across the street from our house, and they would catch minnows to feed his fish in the studio aquariums. One day he let five-year-old Jack hold the jar in which they put the fish, repeatedly warning him not to let go of the jar. When Jack slipped on the step going down into the lake, the jar hit the cement and broke. He valiantly held on to the top, crying, "Daddy, I didn't let go of the jar!"

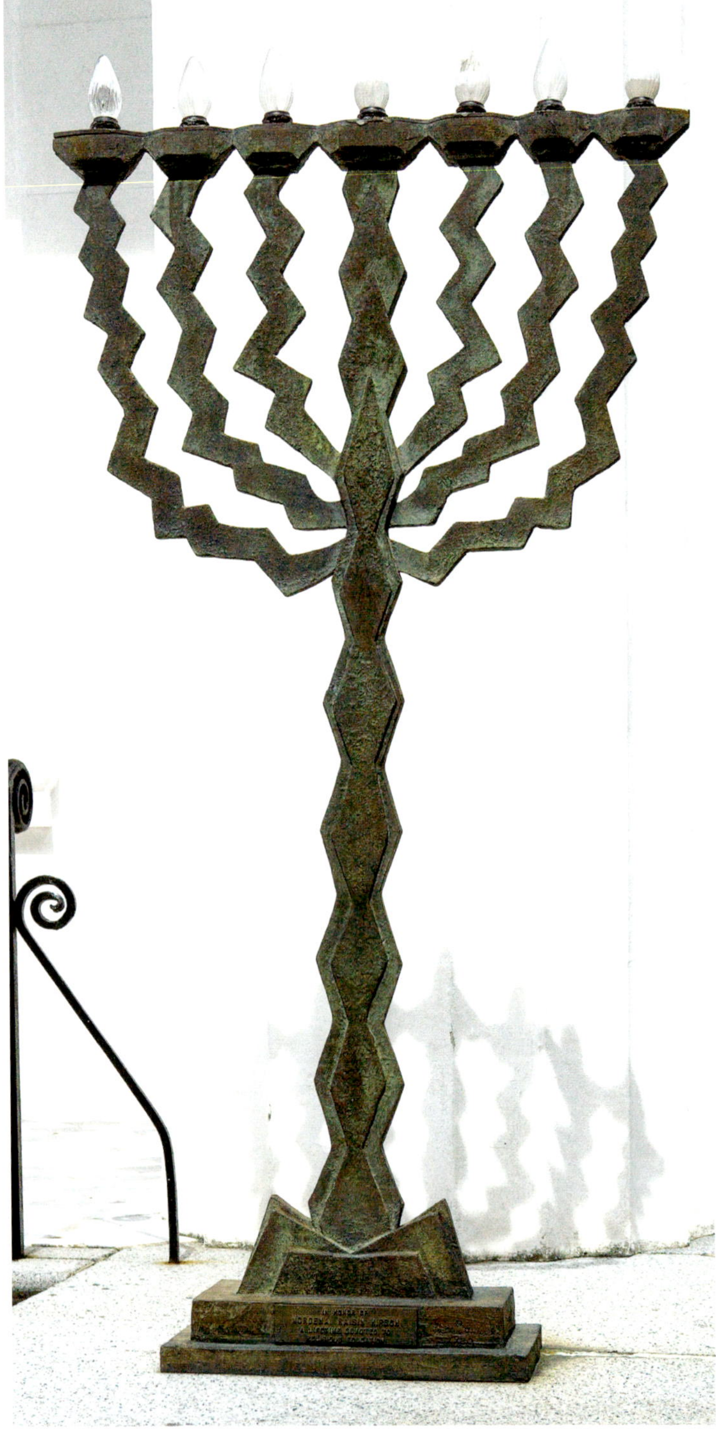

Years later in the 1970s Jack attended the University of Pennsylvania. When we went to the train station to meet him for his freshman winter break, he got off the train with long curly hair, a bushy beard, and a pierced ear. Willard was disgusted and told him to get back on the train and head back north. It was only my begging that made him let Jack accompany us home for the holidays.

Willard loved Charleston. He had many friends and admirers. He died at seventy-seven, due largely to a lifelong habit of smoking. He has been greatly missed, but his many and varied works around our city bring him constantly to mind not only to the family and close friends but also to acquaintances and strangers as well.

Mordenai Raisin Hirsch is a sixth-generation Charleston native who still lives in the house on Broad Street where she grew up. She was married to Willard Hirsch for thirty-three years.

Fig. 28. Willard Hirsch, *Menorah*, 1982. Bronze, 5 ft. 7 in. tall, Kahol Kadosh Beth Elohim Synagogue, Charleston, S.C. Photo by Douglas M. Pinkerton.

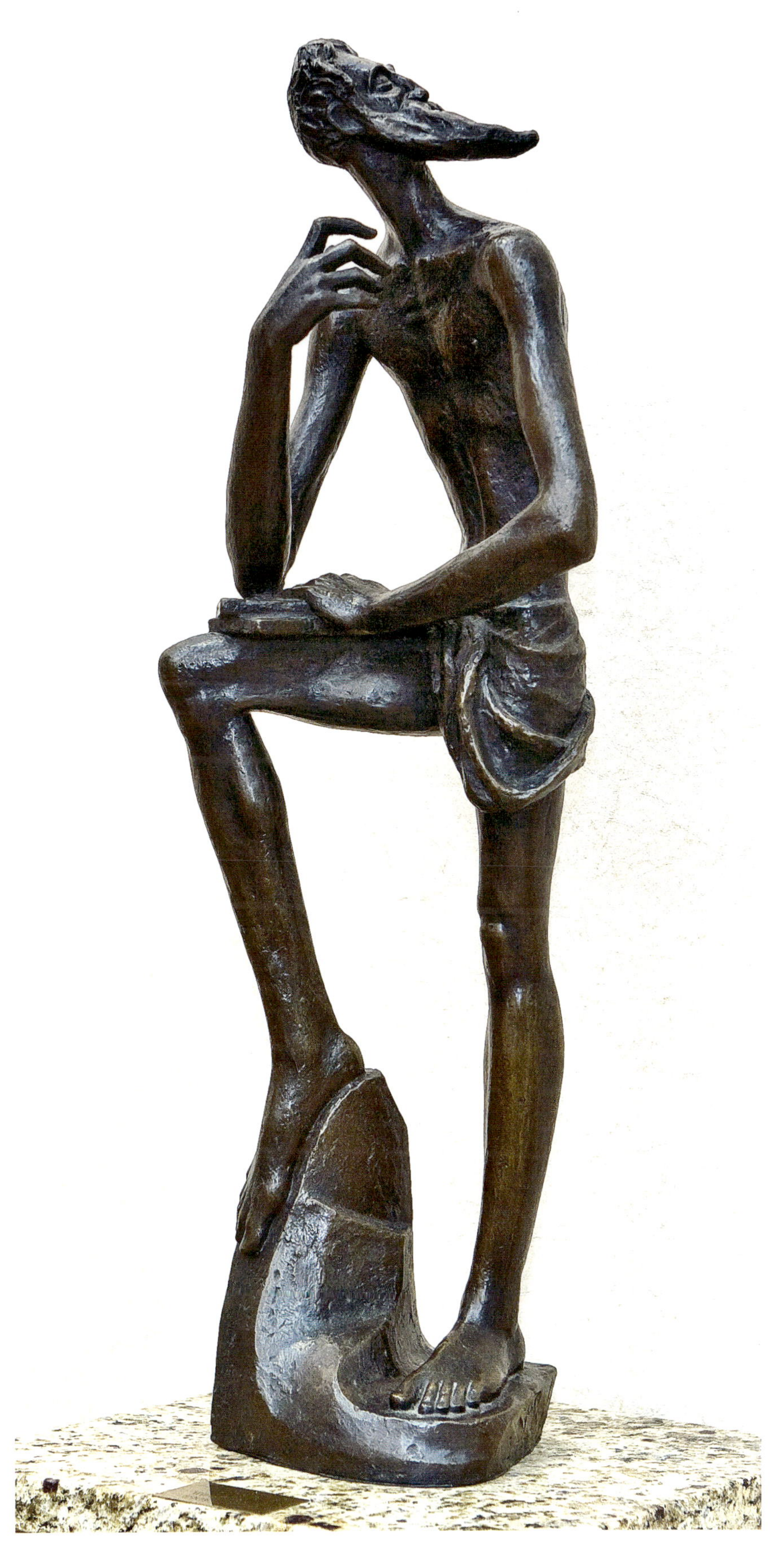

Fig. 29. Willard Hirsch, *Sinai*. Bronze, 30 in. tall, Sylvia Vlosky Yaschik Jewish Studies Center, College of Charleston, Charleston, S.C. Photo by Douglas M. Pinkerton.

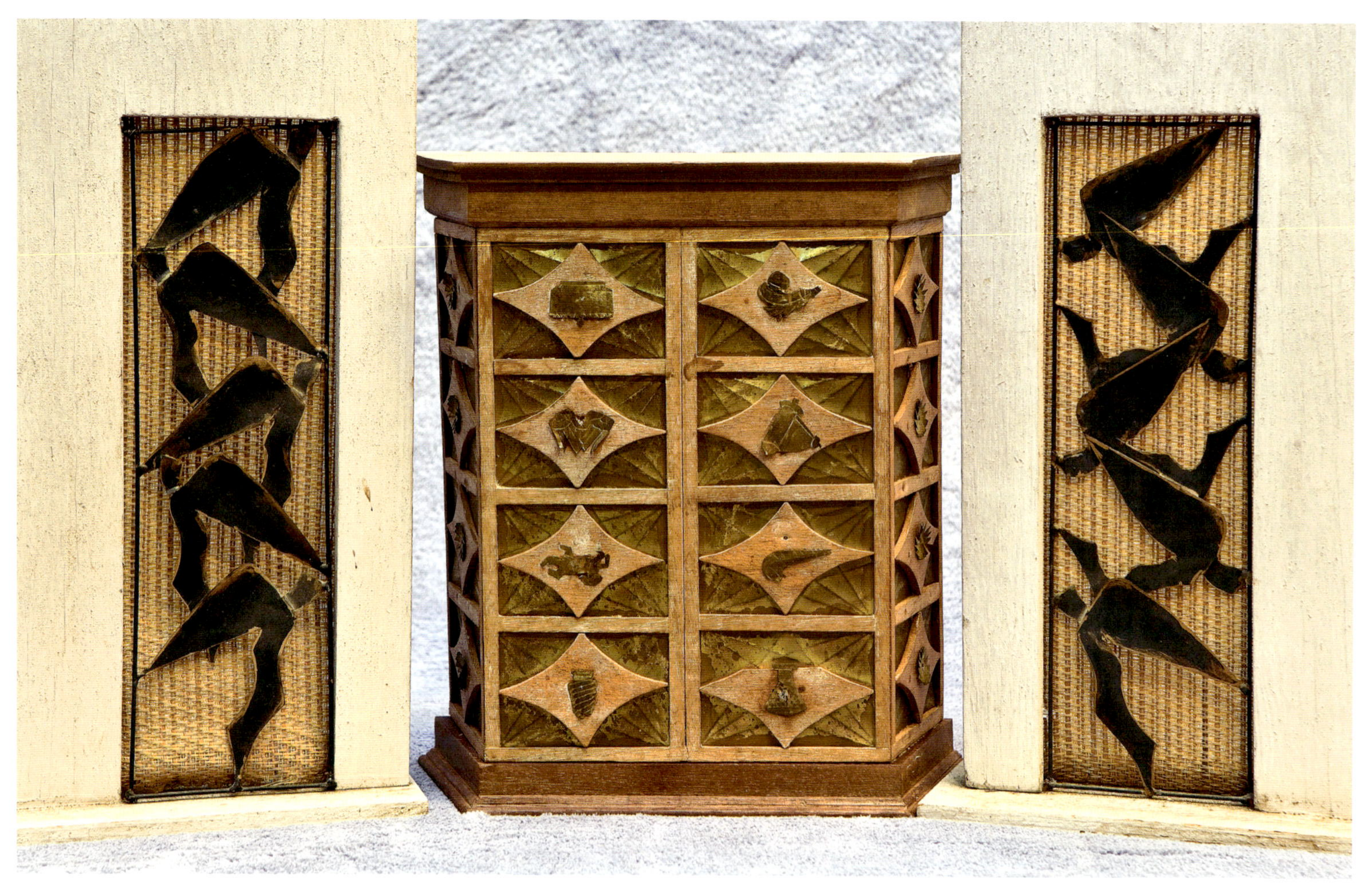

Fig. 30. Willard Hirsch, *Sketch for Ark Screen for Woodsdale Temple* (now Temple Shalom, Wheeling, W. Va.), 1965. Brass, 15 in., Photo by Douglas M. Pinkerton. Special Collections, Marlene and Nathan Addlestone Library, College of Charleston. According to an article in *The Intelligencer* (Wheeling, West Virginia), November 6, 1965, the symbols on the doors of the final version of this ark all depict major Jewish holidays. "The two screens on either side of the altar are allegoric representations of Jacob's Dream as recounted in the Book of Genesis. The rabbis have interpreted that passage to symbolize man's aspirations toward the divine as well as his concern for the matters of this life. In keeping with this theme, one of the panels points upward to divine matters and the other downward towards concerns of this life. Thus, the dual nature of man is symbolized."

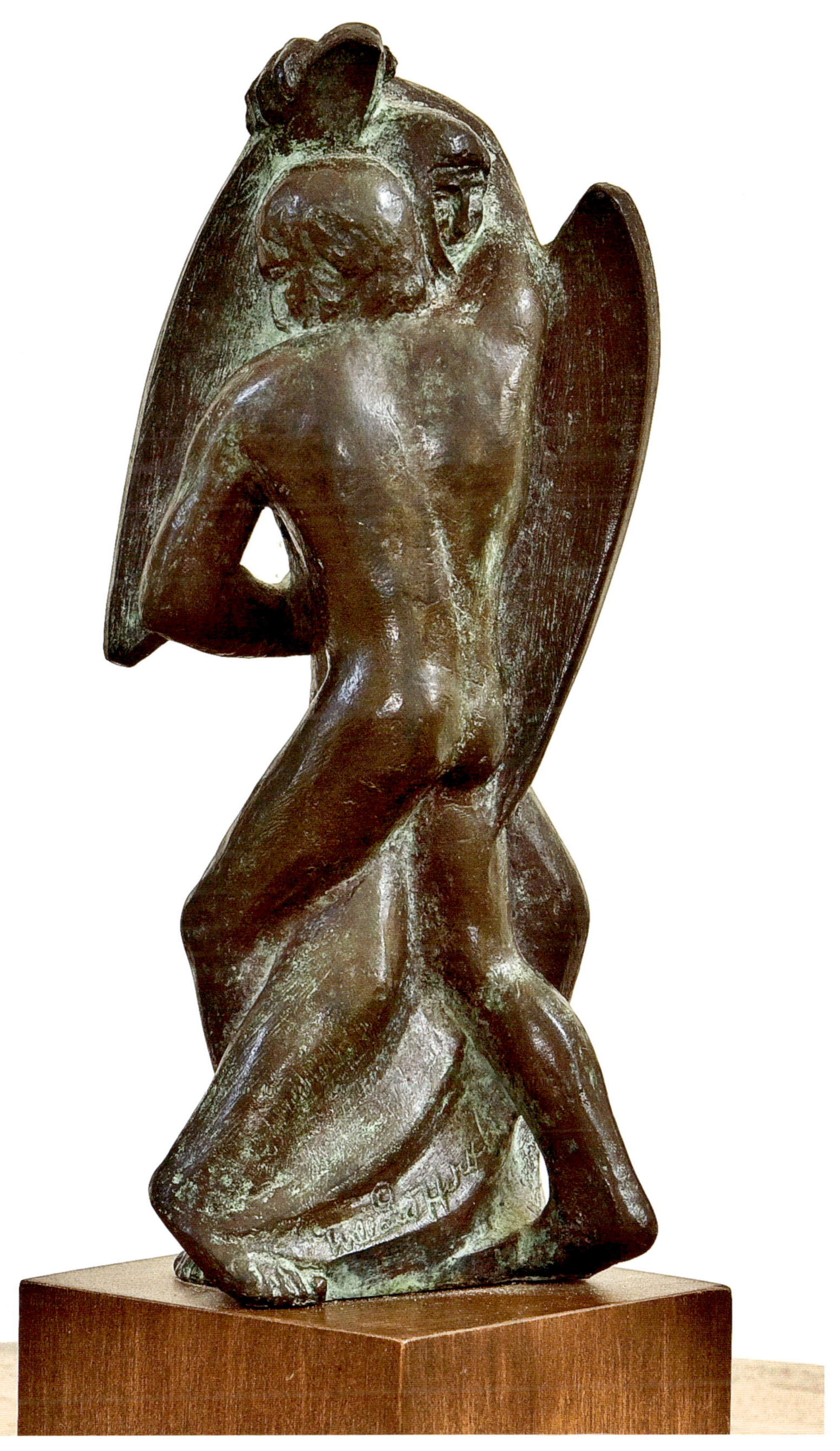

Fig. 31. Willard Hirsch, *Jacob Wrestling with the Angel,* 1959. Bronze, 9 in. tall, Jack and Florence Kurtz collection. Photo by Douglas M. Pinkerton.

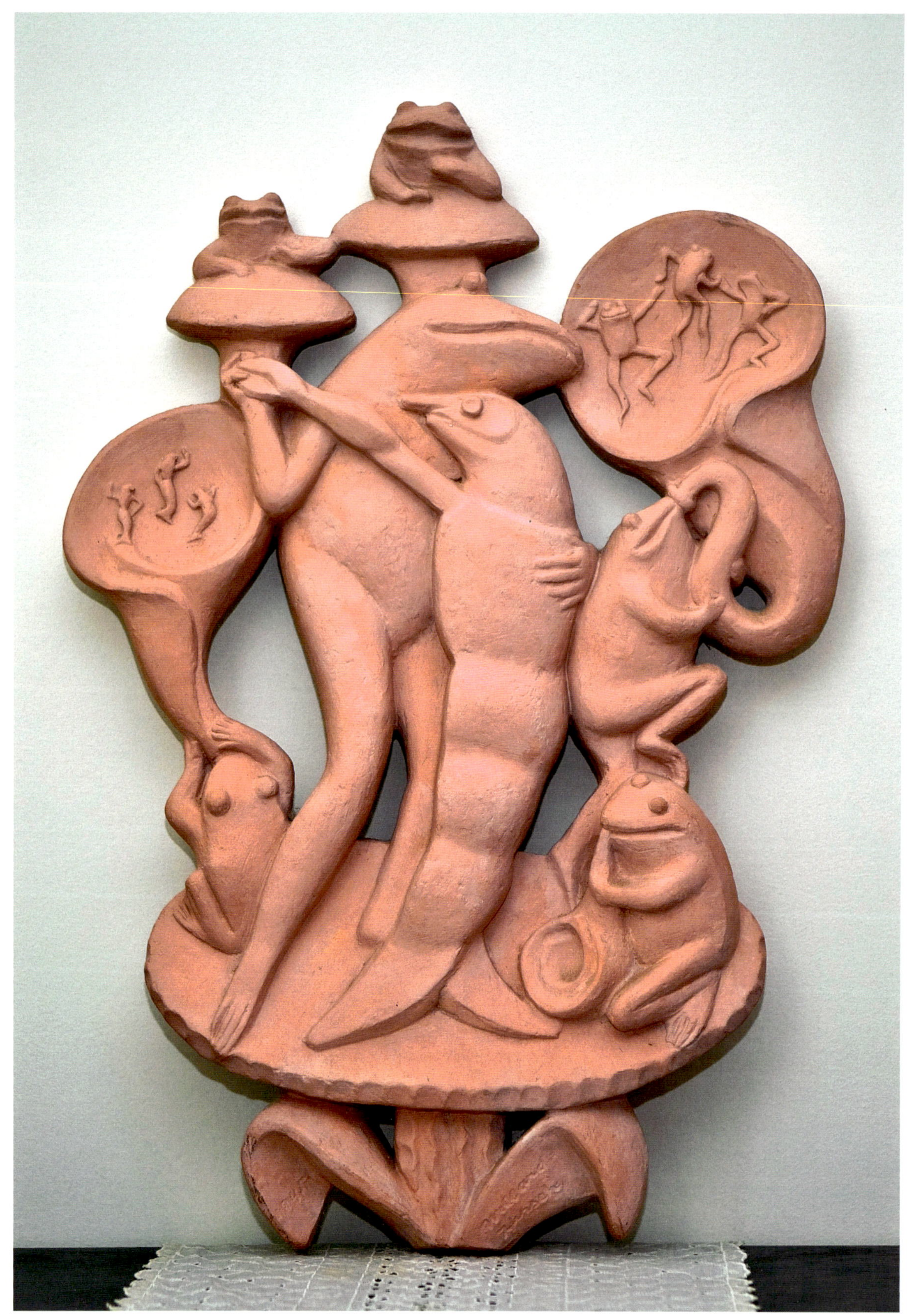

Fig. 32. Willard Hirsch, *Spring*, 1945. Terra-cotta, 23 in. tall, private collection. Photo by Douglas M. Pinkerton.

Making Faces during Prayers

Jane Elizabeth Hirsch

My grandfather, Alexander Abraham (A. A.) Hirsch, wrote a brief biography of the Hirsch family, titled "Lovingly Dedicated to the Sacred Dead." He called his father, Isaac Willard (I. W.) Hirsch, "Mr. Daddy," a habit my father and his siblings continued. I. W.'s father, John Melvin Hirsch, was a native of Stockholm, Sweden, who dreamed of going to America, "the land of the free." So in 1825 he left for America with only his violin and ended up in Charleston, where he met his future wife, Miriam Wolfe. They had two sons, John Melvin Jr. and Isaac Willard. In 1847 they moved to Brownsville, Texas, and then to Matamoros, Mexico, during the American occupation in 1848. Jewish worship was forbidden at that time in Mexico, so the family's attic was a secret place for worship and meetings.

In 1861 I. W. Hirsch joined the Confederate Army at age seventeen. After the war, he returned to Charleston, and in 1873 he married Elizabeth Harris. I. W. was an ardent Jew who belonged to and regularly attended Kahol Kadosh Beth Elohim (K.K.B.E.) Synagogue. He and his family lived at 30 Montagu Street in Charleston, where he died in 1925.

In 1903 A. A. Hirsch married Miriam Newman (*Figure 33*), whom he had met in New York. Their first son, Thomas Newman, died at birth. My father was born in 1905, and then came Roslyn in 1907, Marion in 1909, and Elizabeth in 1912. The family continued to live at 30 Montagu and to worship at K.K.B.E.

Little is known about my father's boyhood and his family. He and his brother Marion shared a wonderful sense of humor, which I assume served them well as children. In 1927 A. A. Hirsch died, requiring my father, who was then twenty-two, to take on many adult responsibilities at a young age.

My parents were married for thirty-three years before my father's death. My mother has always been a gentle person who does not like to raise her voice and never speaks ill of anyone. In contrast, Daddy had a quick temper and spoke his mind, whether his words were offensive or not. Therefore, while he had many admirers, he also rubbed some people the wrong way. My mother was the balance in their relationships with others as

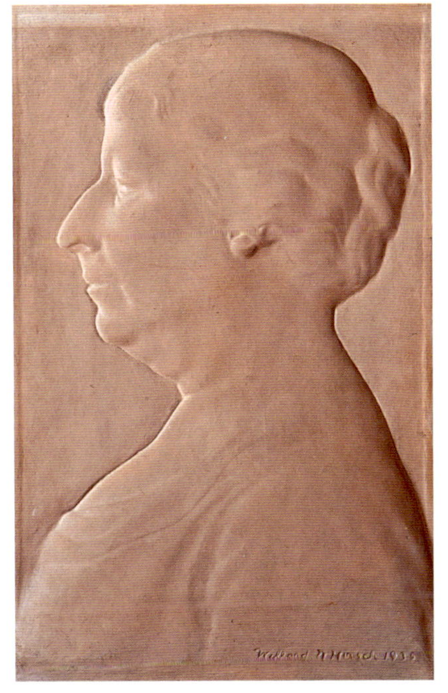

Fig. 33. Willard Hirsch, *Miriam Newman Hirsch*, 1935. Terra-cotta, 14½ in. tall X 9 in. wide, Hirsch family collection. Photo by Douglas M. Pinkerton.

well as within our family. My father and my mother had the same moral values and shared in teaching my brother Jack and me the importance of honesty and integrity. In high school, I gave some younger kids tennis lessons for which I was paid cash. My father insisted on reporting it to the Internal Revenue Service. They also taught us to respect all people, no matter what their religion or the color of their skin. I think my mother's soft-spoken manner and gentleness helped tame Daddy. When she protested one of his tactless outbursts, he often responded with teasing, but he would soften his next words. Her almost-forty years of teaching first grade no doubt gave her the skills to deal with him! Patience is one of her many outstanding qualities, along with a wonderful sense of humor. Not many women would have tolerated their new husbands taking fishing nets on their honeymoon and stopping at roadside ditches to dip for possible aquarium gems!

I was fortunate to grow up in downtown Charleston. When my parents married, my father didn't have much money so he moved into my mother's family home on Broad Street by Colonial Lake. My mother lives there still. Jack and I walked to school (Charleston Day School for me; he went to Memminger and the Gaud School), Mom drove a short distance to the Addlestone Hebrew Academy, and Daddy drove to his studio, about a mile away. We were all at home for a two o'clock dinner and had supper at night, typical of Charlestonians. Mealtimes were always fun. Daddy would taste something and screw up his face as if it were horrible, at the same time drawing out the word "d-e-e-l-i-c-i-o-u-s." When we said grace before eating, he often made faces at me across the table, making me giggle. Daddy was not a morning person; I never saw him before school. The only times he rose early were when he had to fire the kiln. Then he went to the studio very early so it would be ready on his return at a more reasonable hour. After Jack and I went to school, Daddy and Mom had their breakfast. Daddy wouldn't leave the house without his "hominy." Sunday was his day to fix us breakfast—which meant cereal or frozen waffles. He returned home from the studio every day around five and took a twenty-minute nap. I always marveled at how he knew exactly when twenty minutes were up!

For years, Daddy taught children's classes at his studio on Exchange Street, only a few blocks from my elementary school. On Mondays, he picked me up after school, and we went to Robertson's Cafeteria on Broad Street for two o'clock dinner. He always enjoyed a hearty dinner, either meat and potatoes or meat and rice. He claimed that he got his vegetables by letting the cow eat the grass and then eating the cow. He made me feel very grown up by introducing me to his Broad Street business friends who stopped by our table to say hello. After we ate, we returned to his studio for class. One of his rules was: we could only make animals or people—no plants or inanimate objects. I loved his demonstration of how to make a turtle: take a lump of clay, roll it between your hands into an ice cream cone, fat and rounded at one end, narrow and pointed at the other. Next, roll a banana, then a hot dog, and place them on either side of the ice cream cone. Mold a candy apple, a round ball, and place it on top. Gently push down onto the apple and—voila!—a turtle! The round part of the cone was the head, and the pointed end was the turtle's tail; the banana and hot dog were the legs, which stuck out on either side under the candy-apple shell. (In the writings that follow, it's clear that his former students remember the steps slightly differently.) He was very good at making things fun and interesting for us kids. He was a tease, however, and I think he frightened some kids.

Daddy's studio took up the whole upstairs of the building at 17 Exchange Street The front room was where he created his sculptures, taught his classes, and kept his numerous fish tanks. The back room had his finished pieces stored on pedestals and his kiln. As a child I ran about and played hide and seek around his larger pieces. Fortunately, I never broke anything! My father had a quick temper and was never at a loss for words, especially four-letter ones.

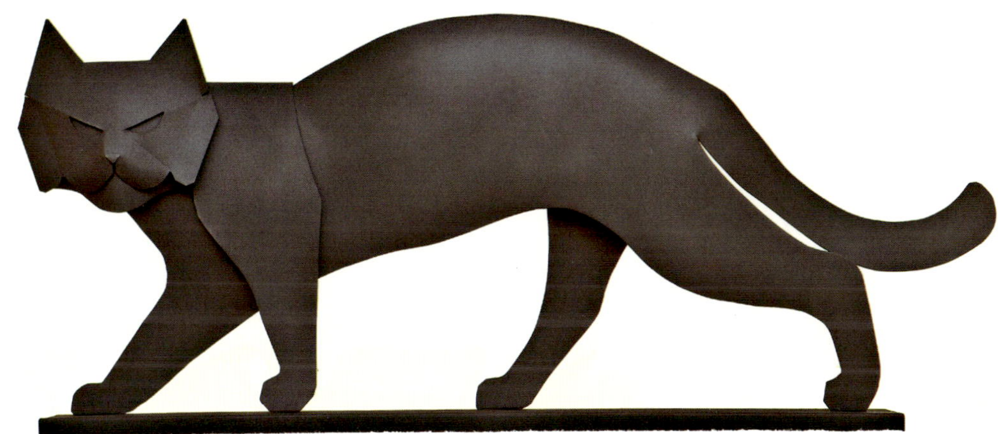

Fig. 34. Willard Hirsch, *Steel Cat*, n.d. Steel, Hirsch family collection. Photo by Douglas M. Pinkerton.

Daddy was an animal lover, something I have inherited from him, and sometimes they have shown up in his sculptures. (*Figure 34)* Many of my early memories involve animals. I begged him for a dog, but he stood firm that I would not be allowed to have one until I was seven years old. When I finally turned seven, he started looking at ads in the paper. He finally settled on a Boston Terrier pup that came with the name of Theodore, so we called him Teddy. It annoyed my mother that after visits to the beach, my father put Teddy and me into the tub together for a bath. He believed in being efficient!

I also asked Daddy repeatedly to take me to a dog show. Soon after we got Teddy, there was one nearby, so off we went. I wanted to pet every dog we saw. There was a Great Dane tied to a tree. I kept asking to pet the Dane, but Daddy said no. Just as I whined, "Why not?" the owner came back and the dog put his paws on the man's shoulders; his head was taller than the man's. My eyes widened and Daddy said, "That's why!"

My father was known for storytelling. He kept my brother and me entertained with his stories of when he lived at 30 Montagu Street with his younger siblings. They had chickens as well as a dog. One day their grandfather, Mr. Daddy, brought them a box with holes punched in it, and of course all the children were excited to know what was inside. To their delight and their mother's distress, it was a baby goat. That goat, more than any other element in his childhood, created wonderful stories for Daddy to tell us, over and over: the time that the goat was napping on the sofa with Daddy, and when his mother leaned down to kiss him, the goat reared its head and got the kiss; the story about the goat and chickens getting into the discarded remains of the spiked watermelon and staggering around the neighborhood. My favorite was hearing about the goat pulling Daddy and his siblings around in a little cart. *(Figure 35)*

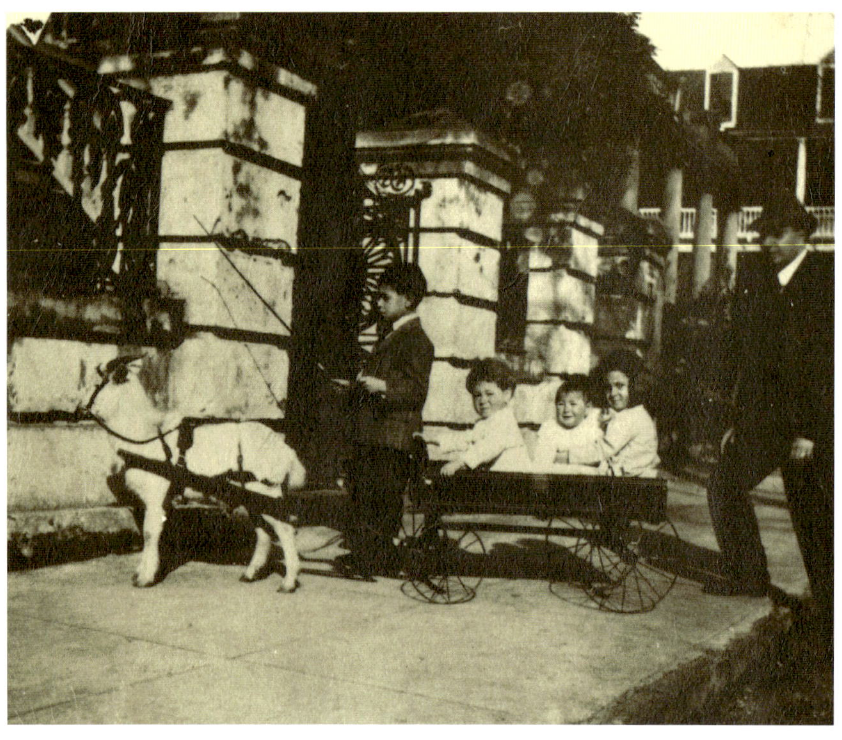

Fig. 35. Hirsch children with goat cart,c. 1912. Hirsch family collection.

I guess because Daddy was allowed to have an unusual pet, he didn't say no when I begged for a baby alligator on sale at Woolworth's for $3.00. I named him Wally and kept him in Jack's bathtub. When Jack took a bath, Wally ran around the bathroom, then was returned to the tub. We caught minnows in Colonial Lake to feed to Wally, and he thrived for a few weeks. When captivity and who knows what else caused him to expire, my father wrapped him up in a cloth and told me he was hibernating and wouldn't wake up until summer. Daddy and Jack made a show of taking him to be released into the wild so he could "finish his hibernation." Years later I learned that they had indeed released the alligator–into the trash at the studio! Fortunately, by summer I had forgotten all about poor Wally!

A friend and I frequently found stray animals, and I wanted to keep every one of them, so Daddy decided to show us what it would be like to have multiple animals. He took us to visit a friend of his who lived in a home that was teeming with cats and dogs, inside and out. The grass needed cutting, there was animal excrement everywhere, and the smell inside could have bowled you over when you walked in. There was no furniture, just bedding and feces all over. We visited briefly and then returned to the car. My father turned to us and said, "Well, girls, see what happens when you have lots of animals?" "We want a place just like that when we grow up!" we chimed in unison.

Once I was in the finals of a local club tennis tournament when Mom was out of town. Daddy offered to watch the match and then take me out to eat, where he could enjoy some forbidden-at-home shrimp. I sat him in between two friends and asked them to supervise him. He asked innocently, "Are you afraid I'll say, 'That's my daughter out there. Who's that dog she's playing?'" He was known on more than one occasion to embarrass us with his bluntness or sense of humor, which not everyone appreciated!

Others, however, have fond memories of my father's humor. Curtis Worthington, one of my brother's friends, has told me that he had his children in stitches retelling Daddy's story of the time he was sailing in Charleston Harbor and fell in, only to be pulled to safety by the Balls–the old Charleston family, that is! Curtis also recalls stopping by our house after a trip to New Zealand, and Daddy asked him if he had seen any marsupials. When my mother corrected Daddy that Curtis had gone to New Zealand, not Australia, my father responded, "Well, it's just across the creek!" Not long after this visit, Curtis brought by his girlfriend, who was wearing a fur coat. Daddy touched her on the sleeve and asked if she were a marsupial!

In 1948 a *Tampa Morning Tribune* reporter asked Daddy why he wanted to catch fish that were only an inch long. He replied that they were worth $1.50 a pair. How did he know if he had a pair, the innocent reporter asked. Daddy replied, "It doesn't make any difference whether we can tell or not, as long as *they* can tell!" The same article related Daddy's story of the baked beans. His habit was to put a can of baked beans on the stove in the studio to heat for lunch. One day he was engrossed in working on a nude study with a live model, and the can exploded. My father was quoted, "If you've never seen a nude model jumping around picking hot baked beans off herself, you've never seen anything."

He could be playful and fun, both in his life and in his sculpture. In 1949 he and my mother went to the Beaux Arts Ball as two of his sculptured angels, and they won first prize for originality! *(Figure 36)* He often sculpted such whimsies as animals playing musical instruments or frogs dancing with crawfish *(See Figure 32).*

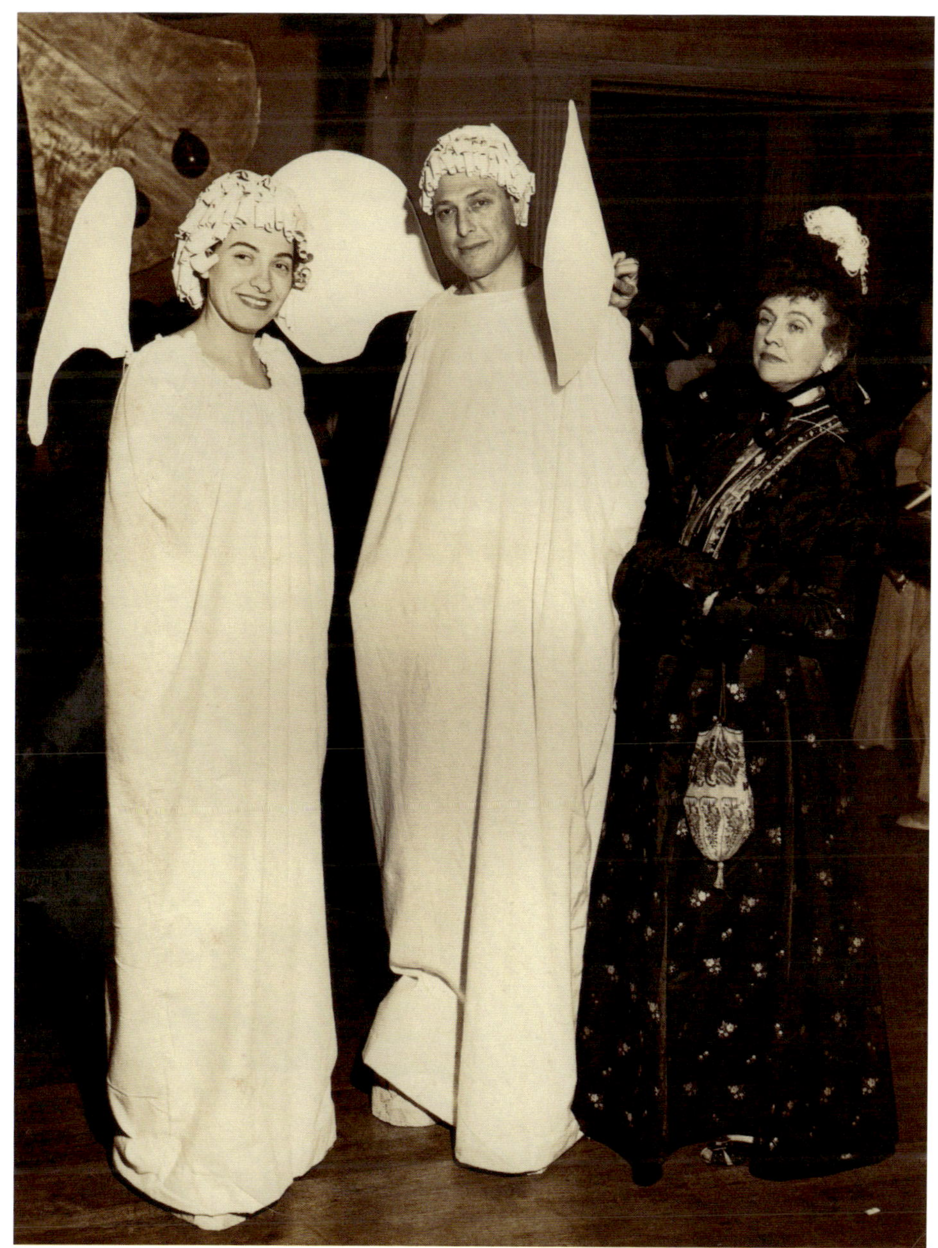

Fig. 36. Mordenai and Willard Hirsch as angels, with Josephine Pinckney, Beaux Arts Ball, November 23, 1949. Photo by Louis Schwartz. Hirsch family collection.

When I was sixteen, Daddy wanted to do a portrait of me wearing the tennis hat that I had worn constantly when I was fourteen. I refused to sit with it on. So, my father played the diplomat and made two heads of me–one with and one without the tennis hat. *(Figure 37).*

My father and my brother Jack were very much alike in their stubbornness and often butted heads. One morning I heard them arguing in the next room, and in typical impatient fashion, my father called my brother stupid. Jack said, "Daddy, I'd much rather hear you tell me you love me than call me stupid!" "Okay, I love you, Stupid!" came the reply.

Daddy often came across as gruff, but he also had a side that not many people saw. I attended Vanderbilt University in Nashville, and was very homesick my freshman year. I remember calling home three weeks before Thanksgiving and telling Mom that I wanted to come home. She was usually the soft touch, but this time she told me to hang in there for

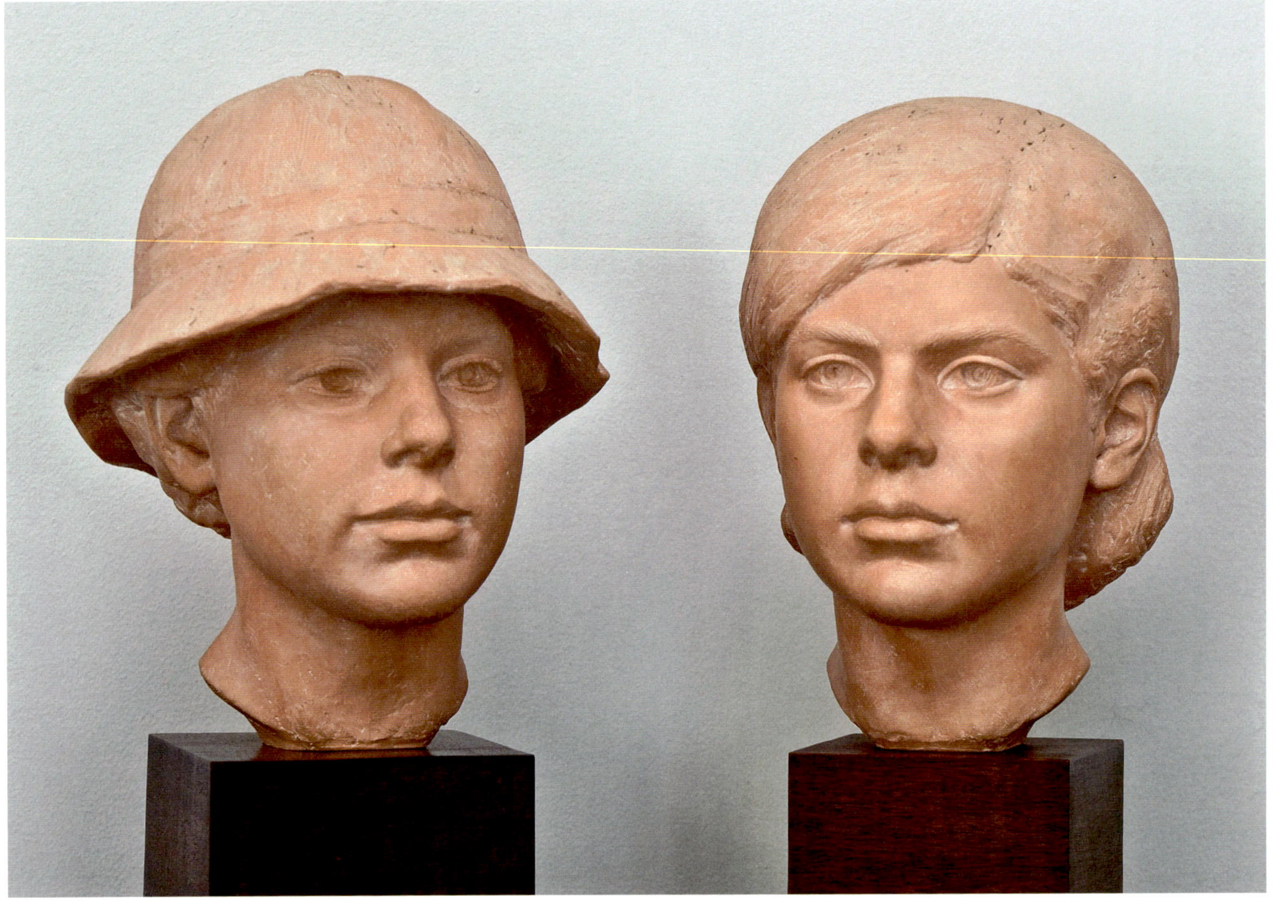

Fig. 37. Willard Hirsch, *Jane with Tennis Hat,* 1972, terra-cotta, 13 in. tall X 12 in. wide, Hirsch family collection, and *Jane without Tennis Hat,* 1972, terra-cotta, 12 in. tall X 10 in. wide, Hirsch family collection. Photo by Douglas M. Pinkerton.

another three weeks. I agreed, but then Daddy took the phone and told me to take a plane out as soon as I could! I came home for a long weekend and was not homesick again throughout my college career.

Though I lived in Florida after graduation, I came home often. A close friend got married, and at the reception Daddy was, well, Daddy. He was talking to the bride's father when a large man stopped to speak to them. As he moved away, my father said in a loud voice, "Mac, who did you say that incredible hulk was?" "My brother!" was the reply!

While Jack and I were becoming young adults, much in our family stayed the same, including our house on Broad Street. It was built in the late 1800s, and Mom's family bought it when she was nine years old. Change was coming, however, both for the better and the worse. In 1978 I traveled for thirteen weeks in Europe playing tennis tournaments, and when I returned Mom and Daddy met me at the airport. That was the start of a new era in our household: Daddy had a moustache *(Figure 38)*, the house was air conditioned, and we had a clothes dryer. While I was in Europe, Daddy had caught pneumonia and, though we didn't know it at the time, that was the beginning of his lung problems.

By 1980 Daddy's many years of smoking were catching up with him. He had emphysema and was often short of breath. Jack and I knew it was serious when we found frozen shrimp dinners in the freezer. During

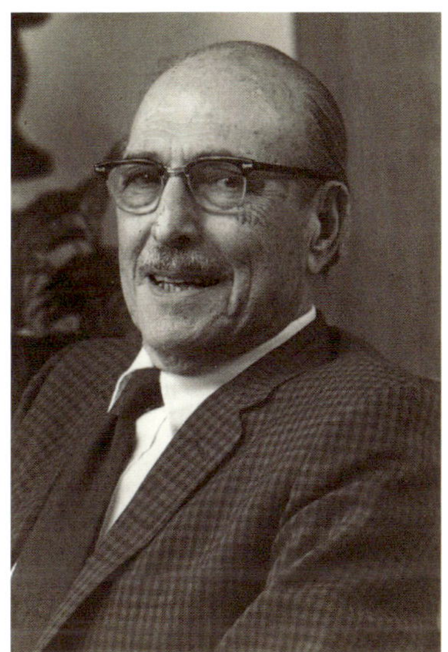

Fig. 38. Willard Hirsch, 1979. Hirsch family collection.

his last couple of years, he was in St. Francis Xavier Hospital several times. I came home from Florida frequently to visit. Once Mom and I were sitting with him in the hospital when the rabbi stopped in to say hello. He asked my father how he was doing, and Daddy embarrassed my mother by saying, "I'm feeling much better now. I'm finally getting some bacon with my eggs in the mornings!"

A few days after Daddy died, on November 30, 1982, Jack Leland of the *News and Courier* wrote, "Shortly before his death, I ran into him in a local hospital where we were both having X-rays made and, although he was in a wheelchair and wearing an oxygen mask, he immediately proceeded to give me a précis on his latest concern, worry over the possibility of one of the many large airplanes using Charleston's airspace falling on the city." He concluded his column, "Willard Hirsch simply didn't have it in his being to back down once he determined that he was in the right. He refused to equivocate where the purity of his art was concerned, and his works speak for his dedication to that purity. He was a rarity in a society that has grown accustomed to compromise, and his like will not come our way again for many moons."

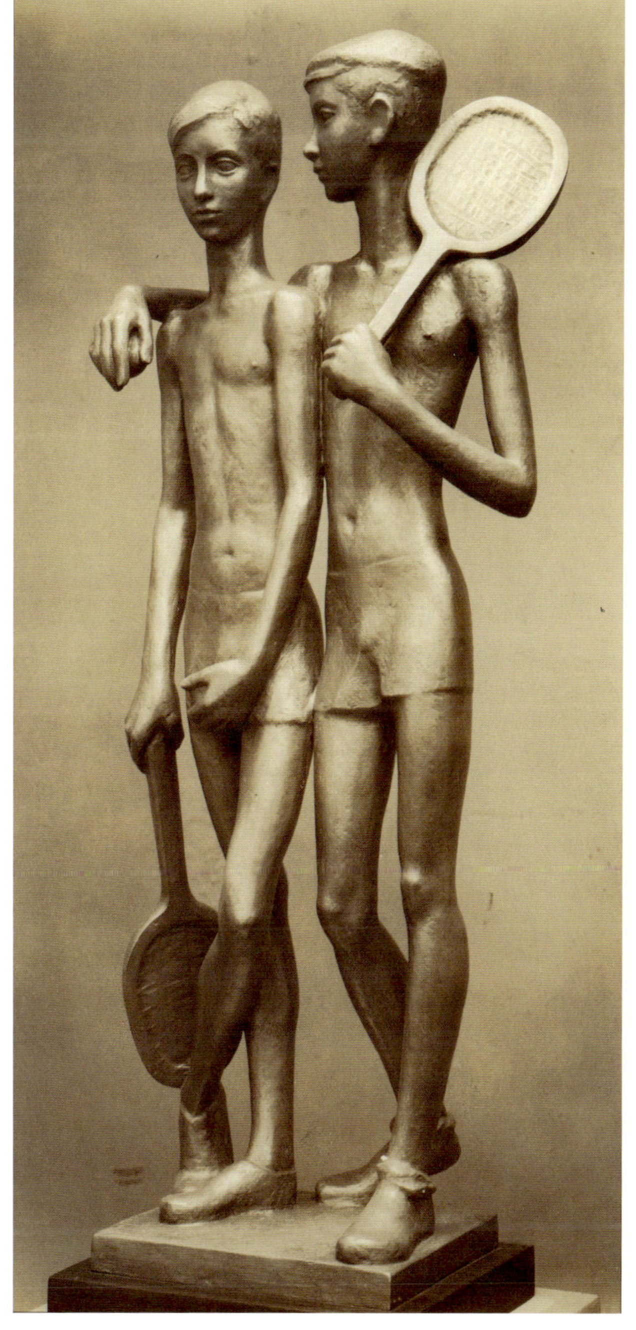

Fig. 39. Willard Hirsch, *Tennis Players*, 1942. Bronze, 36 in. tall, location unknown.

By the time I was born, my father had already made a place for himself in the art world, both locally and nationally. After his studies at the National Academy of Design and the Beaux Arts Institute, he maintained a studio in New York for ten years. Two pieces from his earlier years have special meaning for me, as a sports lover and tennis player. The first was his thirty-six-inch bronze *Tennis Players (Figure 39).* It was commissioned by the International Business Machine (IBM) Corporation to represent South Carolina in the exhibition "Sculpture of the Western Hemisphere." This show featured ninety-seven pieces of contemporary art, one from each state as well Canada and Latin American countries, and traveled widely. In the 1960s this collection was dispersed, and the *Tennis Players* was lost until it was discovered that Estate Galleries in Charleston purchased it in 1995. It sold soon after, and its whereabouts are unknown.

The other sports-related piece that I love is *Sandlot Scrubs (Figure 40)*, a twenty-five-inch woodcarving that he created in 1942. Two boys

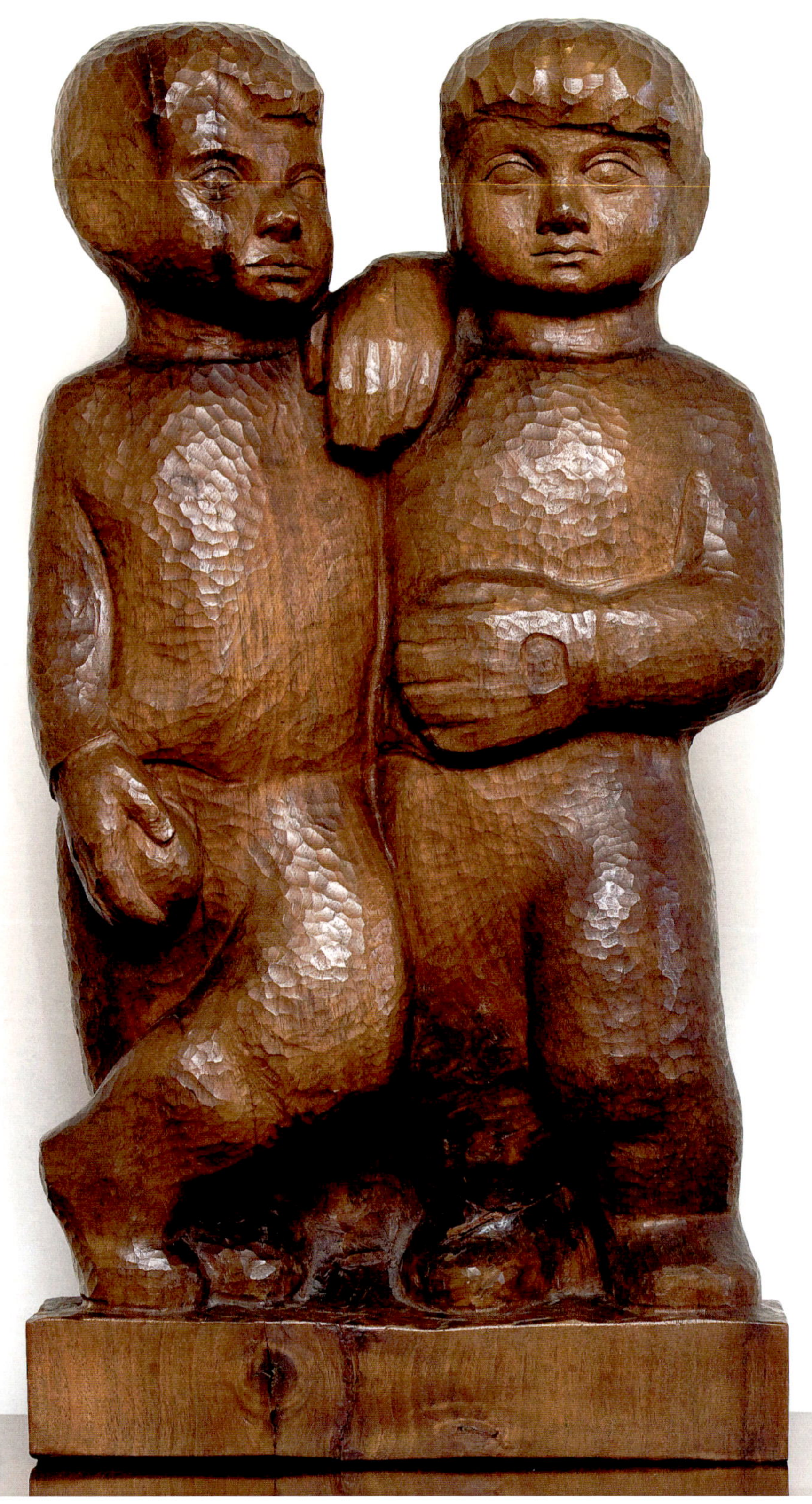

stand side by side, one with an arm draped around the other's shoulders. Their posture suggests the same feelings of camaraderie that I felt before going on the tennis court with a friend. The piece is now in the Bank of America Building in Columbia, South Carolina.

After he got out of the army, Daddy returned to his native Charleston. His second studio was in an old warehouse at 2 Queen Street, which was built around 1840 and had been known as Robert Henry's Warehouse. He turned the downstairs into a large open studio where he could display his sculptures, house his aquariums, and work. He was the first artist of his generation in Charleston to have a kiln, which was in the back storeroom along with his molds. In the front foyer of the warehouse, he placed a bas relief of four bears *(Figure 41)*, because, according to Daddy, "Forebears are very important in Charleston."

In 1947 he joined the faculty at the University of South Carolina and taught classes during the summer sessions for several years. As a teacher he was passionate about his subject. In a 1947 Carolina Art Association publication, he wrote, "The most important function that classes in sculpture can perform, both for adults and for children, is to increase awareness and add to delight in all sculptured objects. Such an awareness is our doorway to living more fully and more richly." Teaching was particularly rewarding

Fig. 40. Willard Hirsch, *Sandlot Scrubs*, 1942. Walnut, 25 in. tall, Bank of America headquarters, Columbia, S.C.. Photo by Douglas M. Pinkerton.

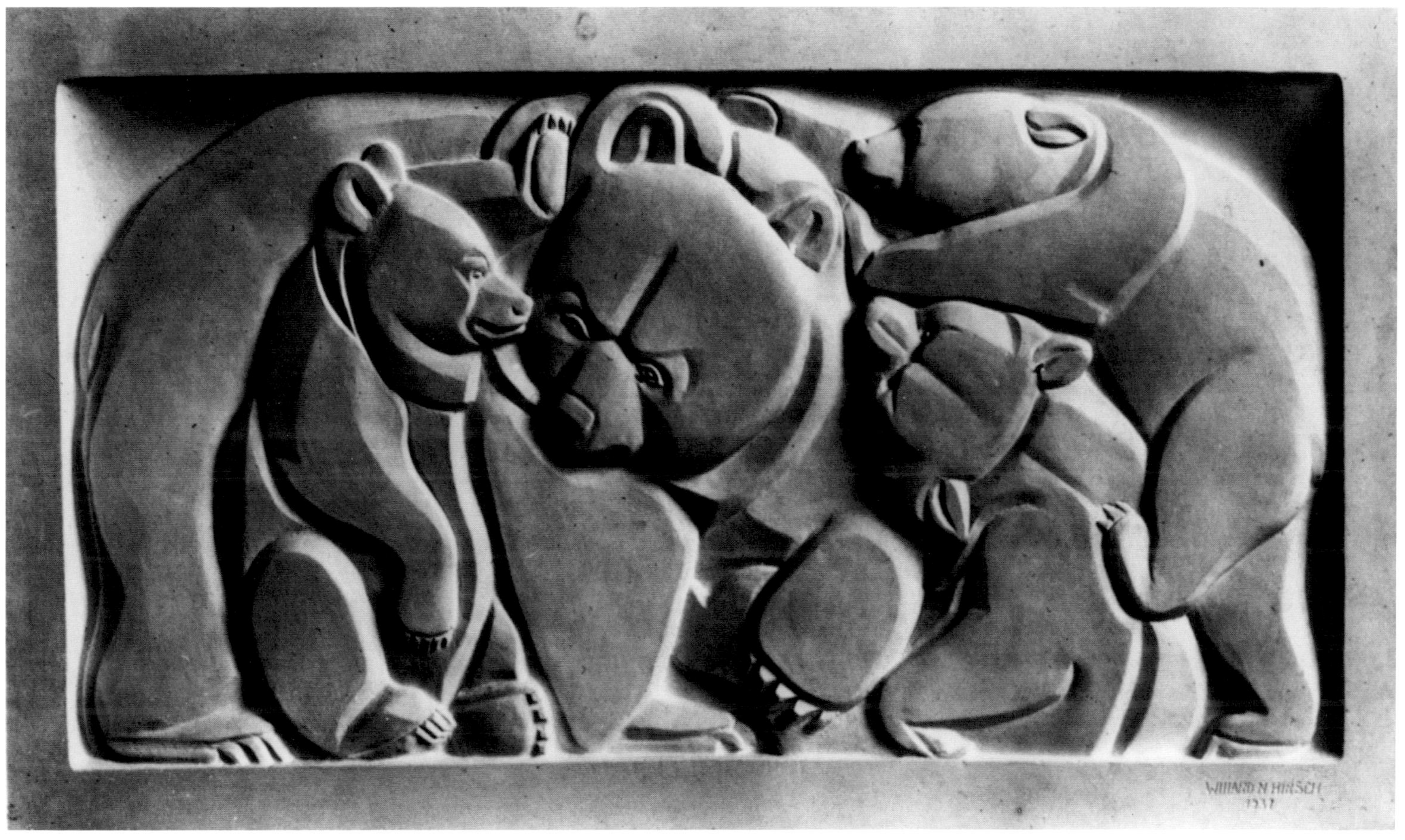

Fig. 41. Willard Hirsch, *Bear Family*, n.d. Terra-cotta, 20 in. tall, Office of the Bureau of Child Guidance, New York City. Photo by Louis Schwartz.

for him because as a young boy he had been interested in sculpture, making figures out of pastilene, but became frustrated and gave it up because there was no instruction or help available. In 1969 he wrote, "I feel that my residence in Charleston makes it unnecessary for any interested young person in the community to postpone his career for lack of instruction."

One of my favorite woodcarvings was a thirty-two-inch walnut sculpture, *God's Children* (see *Figure 26)*, a depiction of an African American baptism. Daddy used the natural shape of the wood and its coloring to create a powerful depiction of the religious ceremony. I remember the story of a minister from Tennessee who arrived on his bicycle to see Daddy's work and fell in love with *God's Children*. The man didn't have the money to buy it, so Daddy let him pay for it in monthly installments. They kept in touch for years.

In 1953 Daddy was commissioned to create a bas relief to go on South Carolina National Guard armories *(Figure 42)*. The four-by-six-foot sculptures were cast in composite stone and depict an American eagle above a palmetto tree and a number of soldiers, dressed in the various military uniforms of the Indian wars, the Revolution, the Mexican War, the War Between the States, the Spanish-American War, the Mexican Border Campaign, World War I, and World War II. Twice this piece has been the center of controversy and made the news. The first time was in the 1960s. A young soldier was ordered to paint the sculpture bright colors.

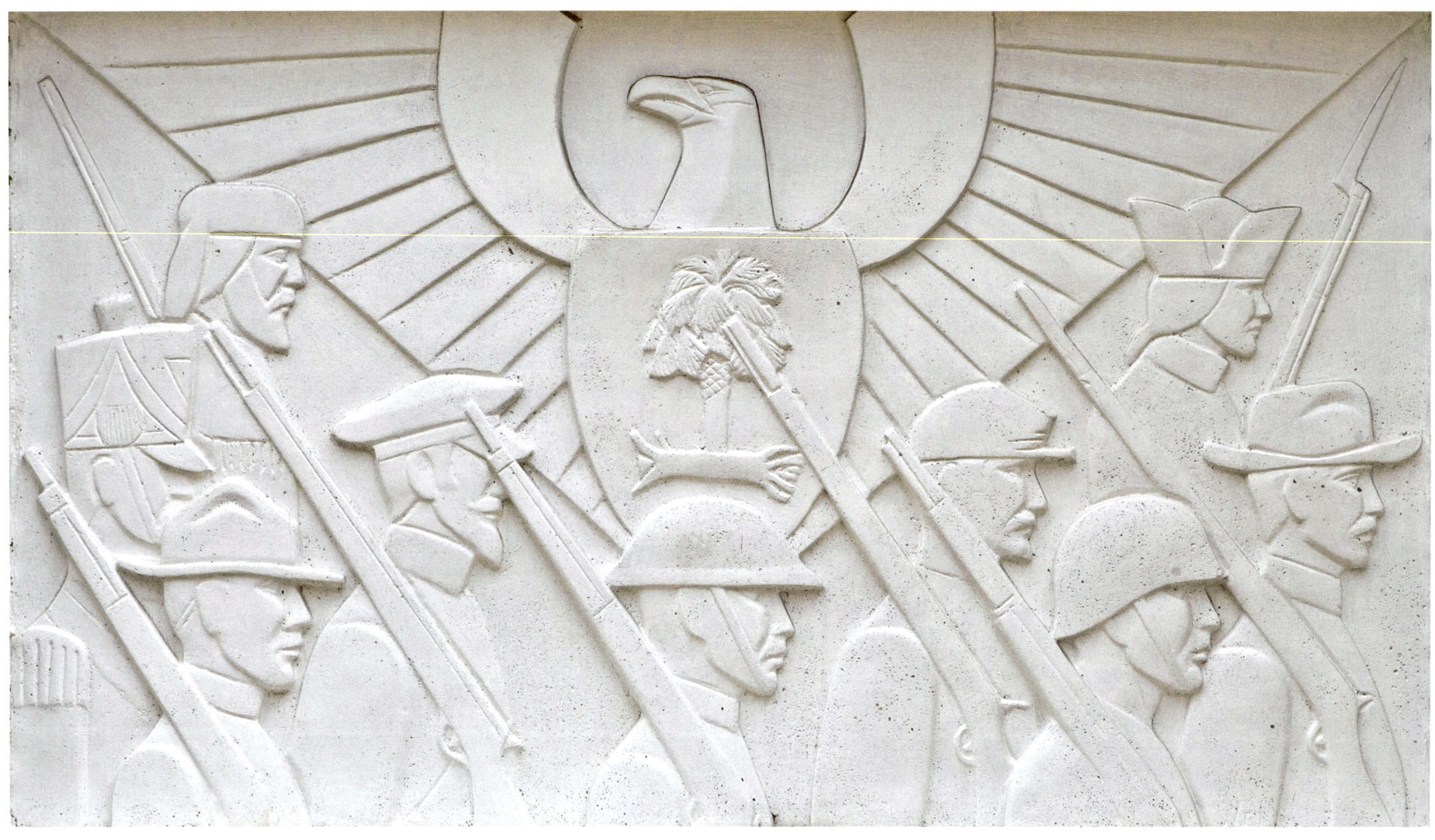

Fig. 42. Willard Hirsch, *National Guard Armory bas relief*, 1953. Composite stone, 4 ft. tall X 7 ft. wide. Photo by Douglas M. Pinkerton.

Daddy was furious and threatened to picket the governor. Eventually, the National Guard agreed to remove the paint. Unfortunately, the removal was done by sandblasting, and even to this day the pit marks and holes can be seen.

In the summer of 2010 a passerby who happened to be an art lover noticed that the sculpture was missing from one of the armories and reported it to the police. It turned out that some soldiers had removed it for safekeeping, as this particular armory was scheduled to be torn down. It is now in storage until a new armory is built and it can be reinstalled. My father would have enjoyed this second adventure of the bas relief!

Daddy did several versions of *Jonah*. One hangs on my wall, a wonderful steel whale with a happy grin and Jonah crouching in its mouth *(Figure 43)*. Like *Jonah*, many of Daddy's works were from Bible stories, including *Jacob's Dream (Figure 44)* or *Jacob Wrestling with the Angels* (see *Figure 31)* In a 1955 biographical sketch he wrote that he had a "deep interest in the universal appeal of the romance of Biblical characters. . . . I feel that the synagogue is the natural patron of the Jewish sculptor just as the Church was of its artists during the Renaissance."

By far, Daddy's best-known and most-loved piece is the *Little Dancer*, the frolicking girl with a toe sticking out near the water of a drinking fountain (see *Figure 20)*. This statue was created in 1955 from an earlier

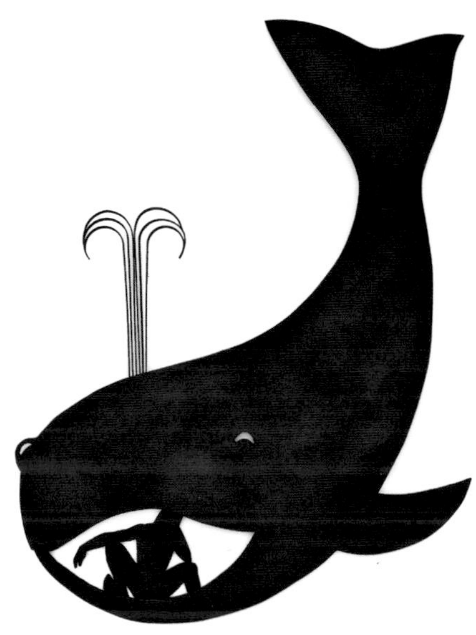

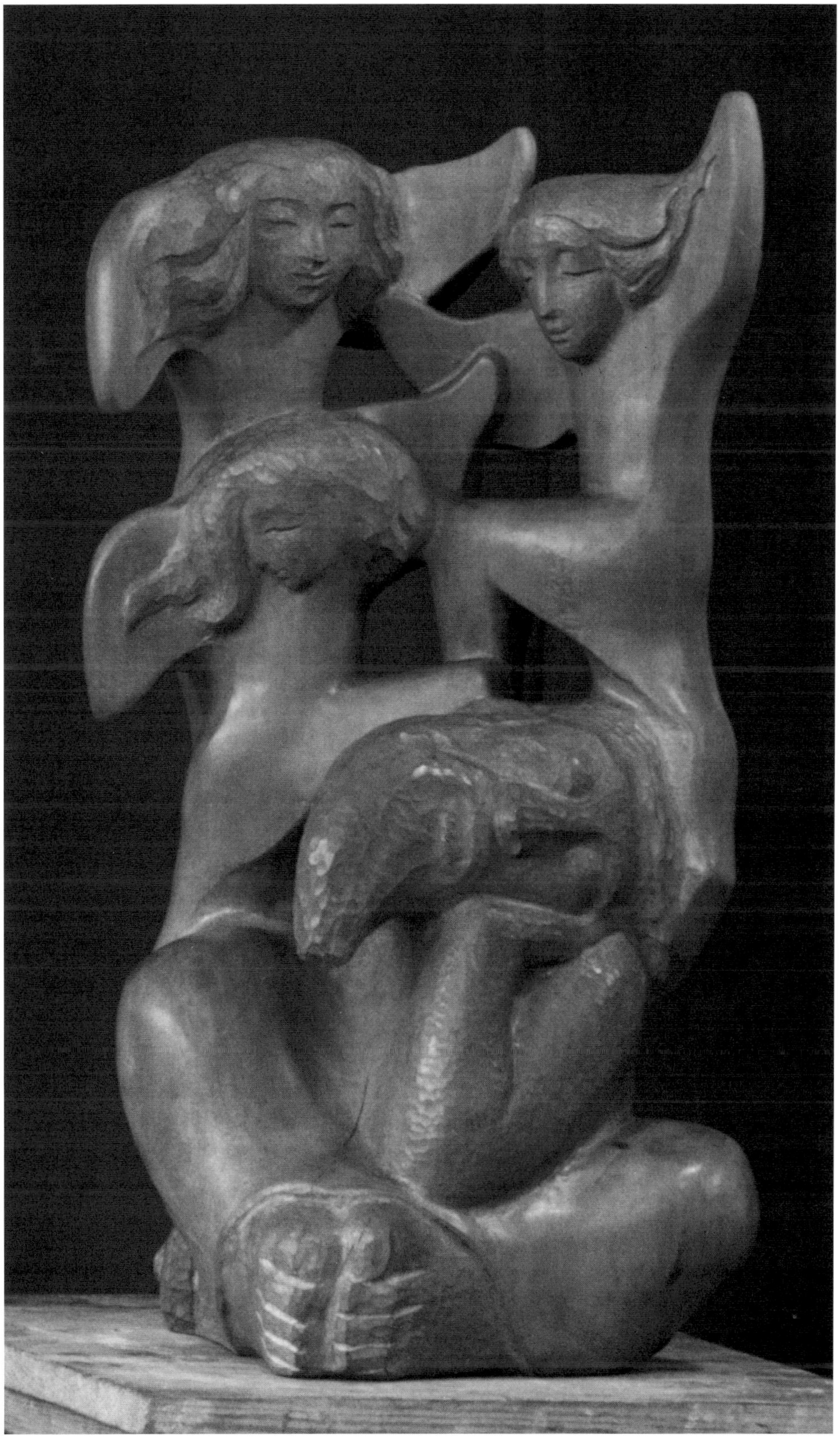

Fig. 43. Willard Hirsch, *Jonah,* n.d. Steel and wrought iron, 36 in. tall, Hirsch family collection. Photo by Douglas M. Pinkerton.

Fig. 44. Willard Hirsch, *Jacob's Dream,* 1949. Planewood, 27 in. tall, Columbia Museum of Art, Columbia, S.C. Photo by Louis Schwartz.

sketch. In 1962 it was donated by a friend to the children of Charleston and installed at White Point Garden. The following year, the *Little Dancer* disappeared. The police were notified, and a reward was offered for the return of the statue. There were no clues as to what had happened to her. Finally, a reporter asked Daddy if he had any comment on the disappearance. He had plenty to say! He had noticed that a bolt holding up the little girl was broken, so he had taken her to the studio for repair.

In 1974 Daddy was commissioned to create a bulldog for South Carolina State College in Orangeburg. *(Figure 45)* He became especially proud of this work after a friend

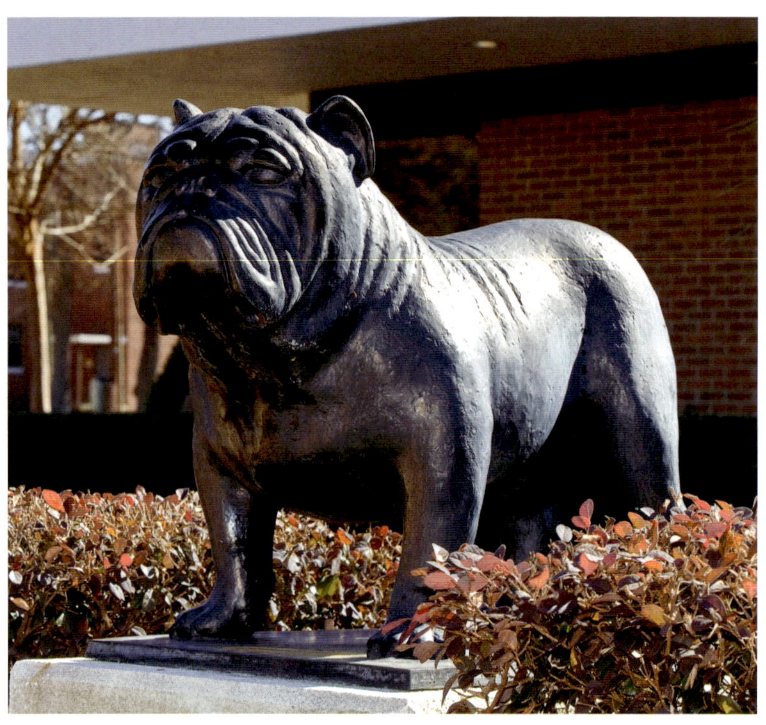

stopped by the studio with his dog and the dog barked and carried on at the statue. Daddy felt that this confirmed the likeness of the piece.

Many of Daddy's pieces had stories that went along with them. He created an angel holding a child in her outstretched arms—just to show that angels can have babies! *(Figure 46)* And there is a pair of angels where the boy is in heaven kicking up his heels in glee because, according to Daddy, he just saw his girlfriend and had been afraid that she wasn't going to make it! *(Figure 47)*

Parents of a young girl who had died commissioned him to create a memorial piece for her school, Ashley Hall in Charleston. This sculpture is called *The Little Angel* and

Fig. 45. Willard Hirsch, *Bulldog*, 1977. Bronze, 21 in. tall X 31 in. long, South Carolina State University, Orangeburg, S.C. Photo by Douglas M. Pinkerton.

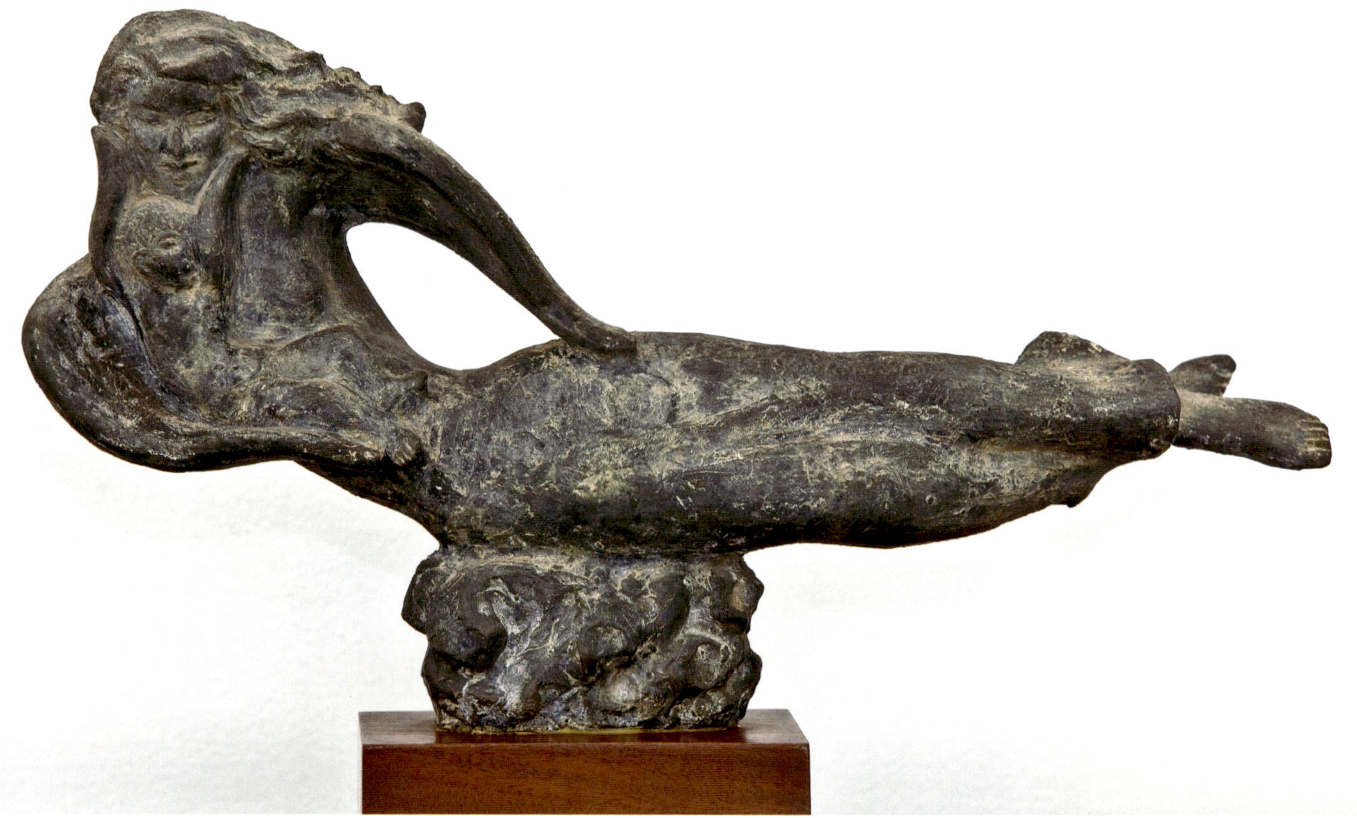

Fig. 46. Willard Hirsch, *Angel Mother,* 1967. Terra-cotta, 9 in. long, Hirsch family collection. Photo by Douglas M. Pinkerton.

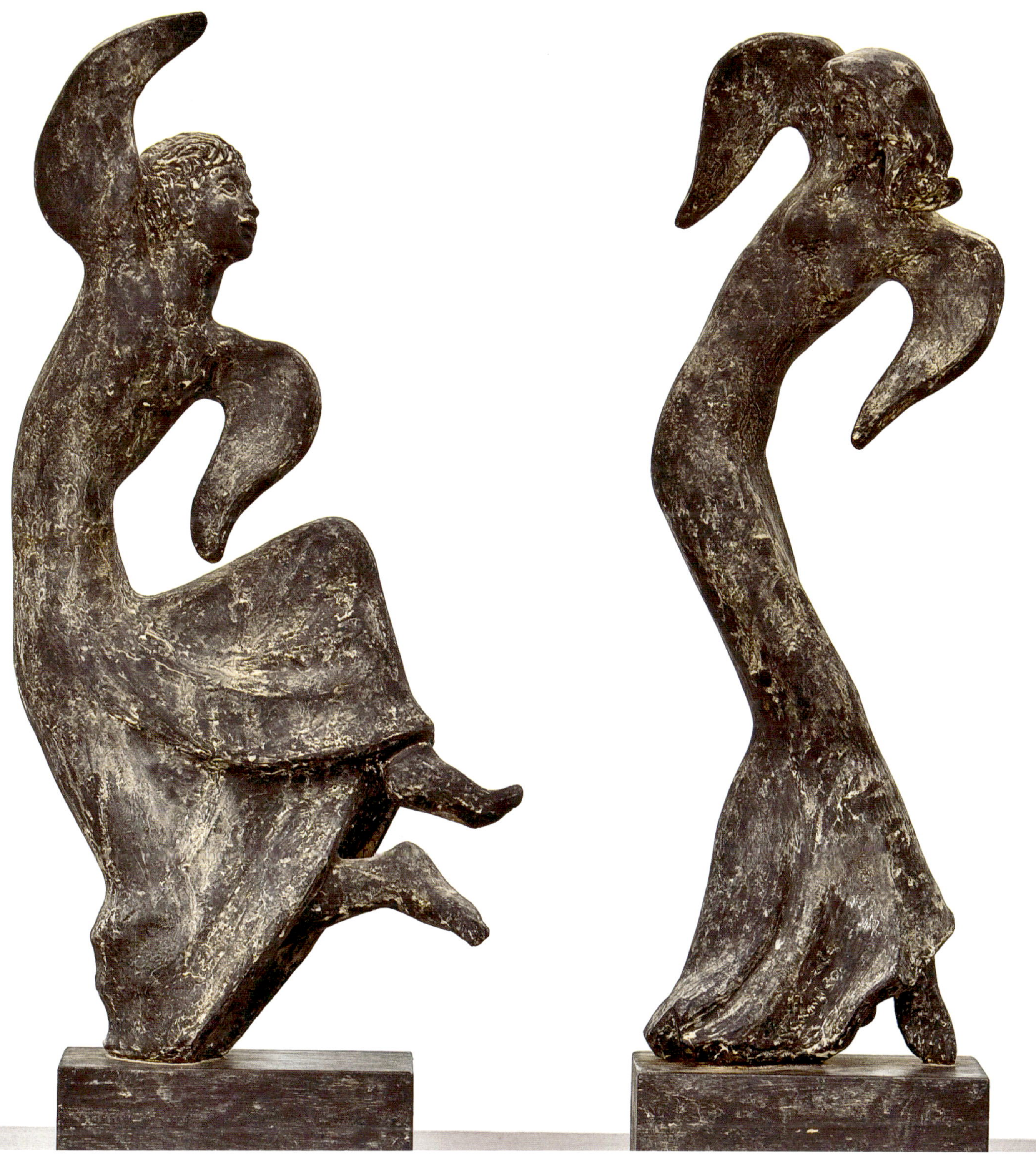

Fig. 47. Willard Hirsch, *Dancing Angels,* 1967. Terra-cotta, 15 in. tall, Hirsch family collection. Photo by Douglas M. Pinkerton.

consists of a little girl's face, arms, and wings, with her hands cupped for water to run through like the ebbing of her young life. *(Figure 48)*

The theme of motherhood can be seen in many of his pieces. *(Figures 49* and *50)* He recognized and celebrated the bond between mothers and children. "My 'mothers playing with children' date back to my student days," he told the *Wilmington* (N.C.) *Morning Star* in 1967. "We had to undergo a tremendous background of religious Madonnas. They were all very solemn. I wanted to portray happy mothers with their children. Motherhood will never go out of style."

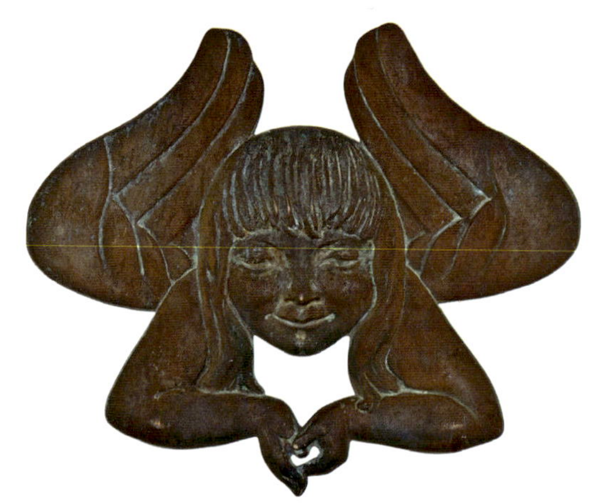

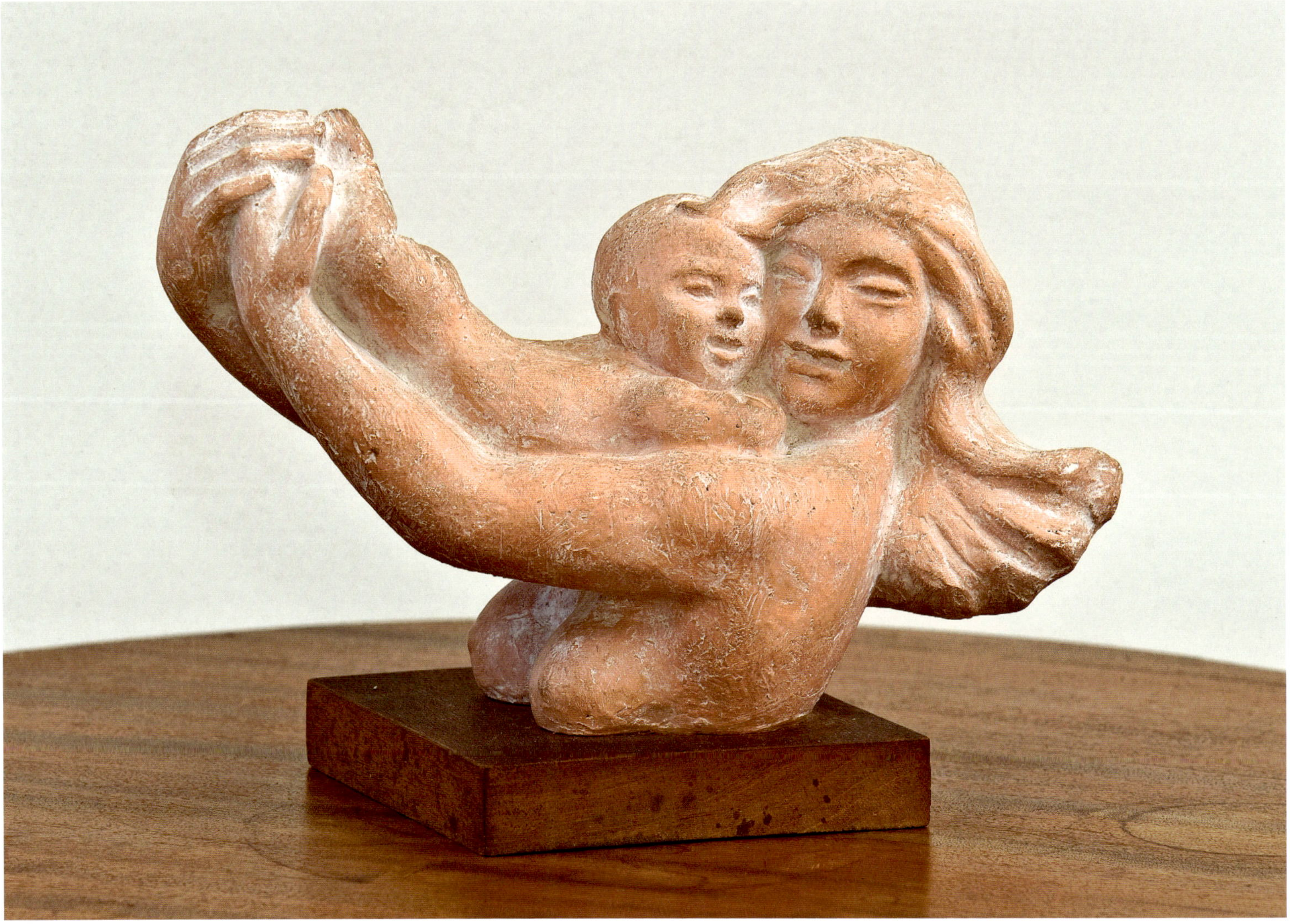

Fig. 48. Willard Hirsch, *The Little Angel,* 1967. Bronze, 20 in. tall, Ashley Hall School, Charleston, S.C. Photo by Douglas M. Pinkerton.

Fig. 49. Willard Hirsch, *Maternity #3.* Terra-cotta, 6 in. tall, Jack and Florence Kurtz collection. Photo by Douglas M. Pinkerton.

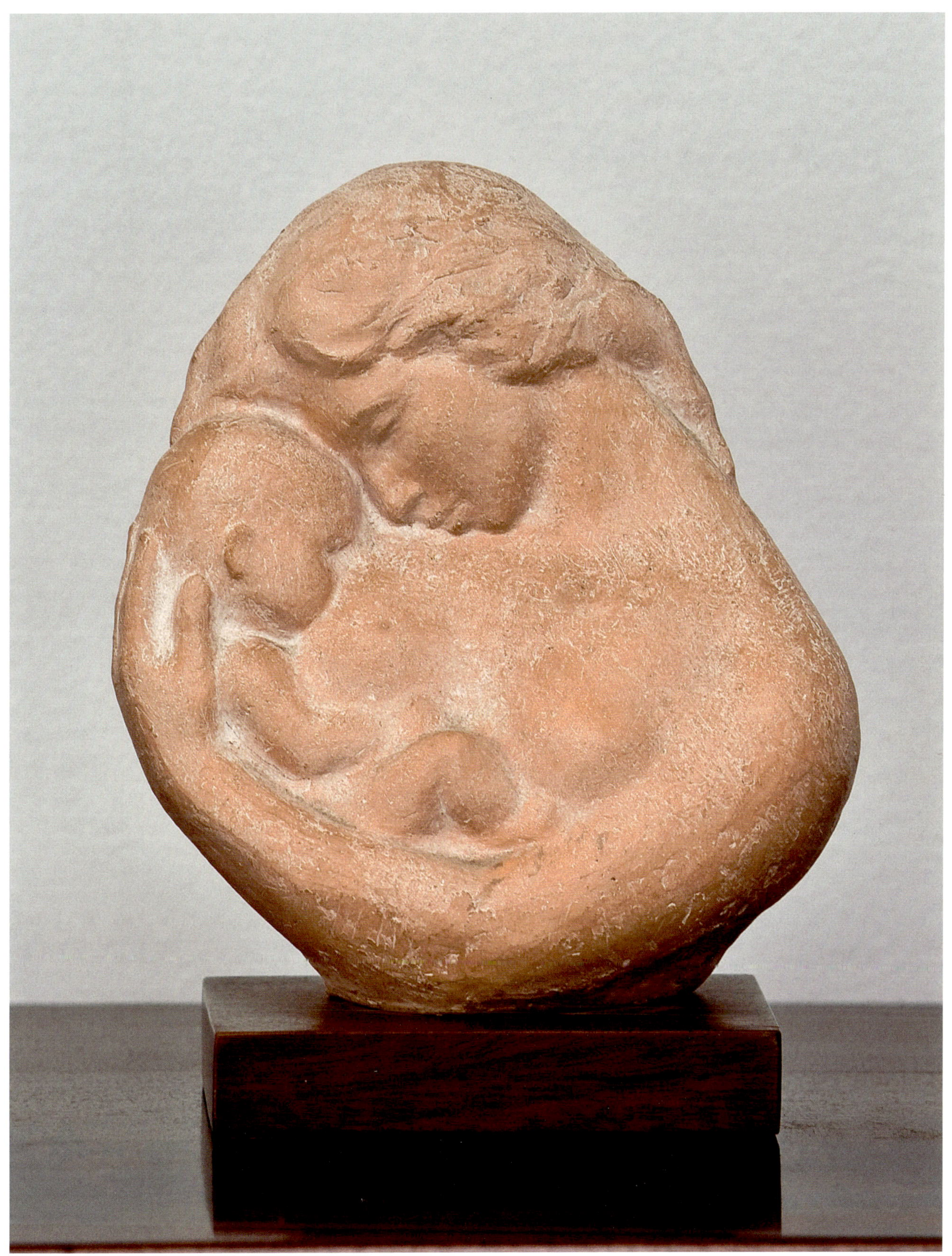

Fig. 50. Willard Hirsch, *Maternity #4.* Terra-cotta, 7 in. tall, Hirsch family collection. Photo by Douglas M. Pinkerton.

In 1970 the Home Federal Savings and Loan commissioned Daddy to create a piece for a fountain in their lobby. While he was working on it, a tennis friend of mine stopped by the house wearing flip flops. As she sat with her legs crossed, feet dangling, Daddy asked if she would come to the studio so he could model her feet! This became the *Joy of Motherhood* and remained there until the bank became Community FirstBank. The statue was given to Ashley Hall for its new Fine Arts building *(Figure 51)* in 1993. While still at Home Federal, permission was given for another casting to be made to be donated by my mother to Brookgreen Gardens in Murrells Inlet, the largest outdoor collection of American figurative sculpture in the country. My father would have been very proud to have a piece of his work exhibited there.

One piece that I cherish is of two pelicans, one hovering over the other *(Figure 52)*, because it was the last sculpture Daddy created. After he died, my mother and I went to the studio and found it on his work pedestal, finished but not fired, and covered in plastic to keep it from drying out. The foundry in Atlanta that Daddy had used for a number of years made two bronze statues before destroying the mold.

I am fortunate to have many memories of my father, both tangible in the sculptures he created and intangible in the loving memories I hold in my heart.

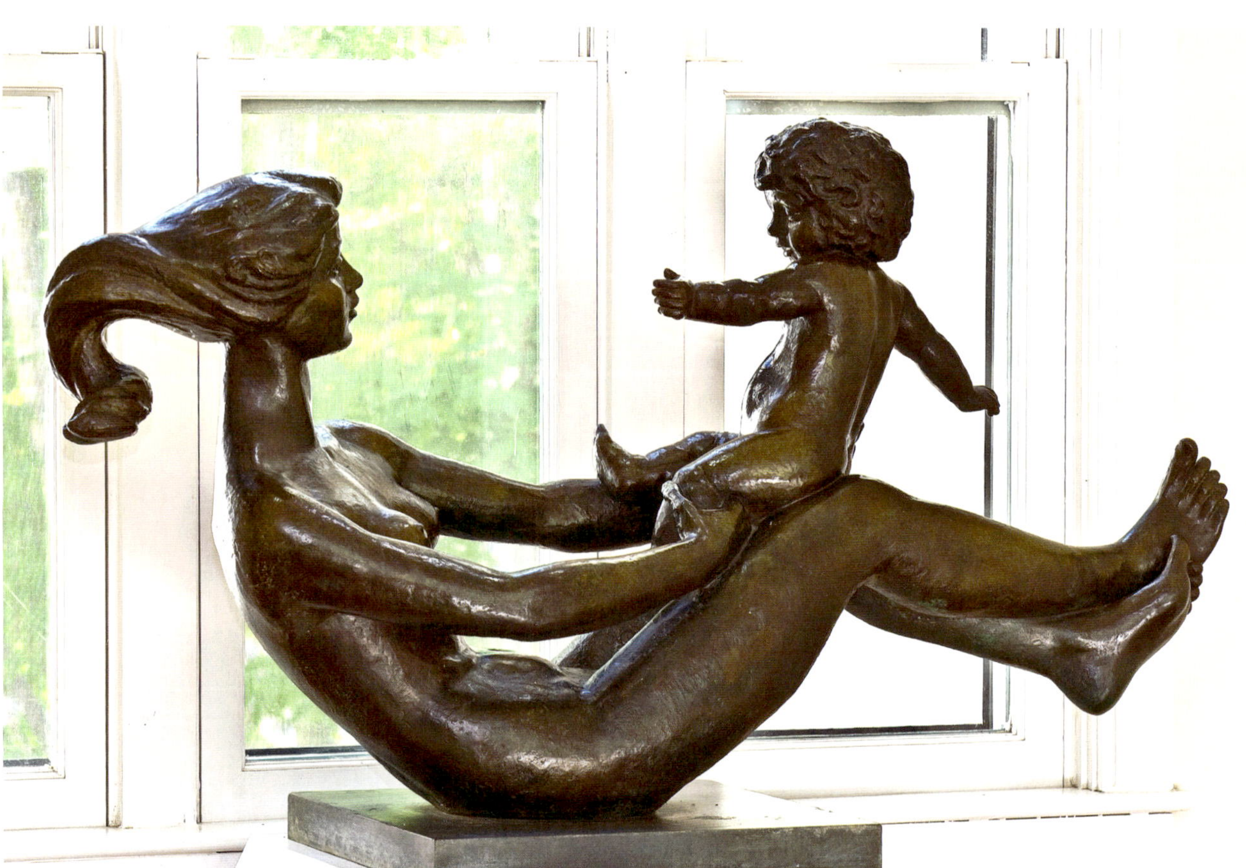

Fig. 51. Willard Hirsch, *Joy of Motherhood,* 1970. Bronze, 29½ in. tall X 56 in. wide X 15 in. deep, Fine Arts Building, Ashley Hall School. Photo by Douglas M. Pinkerton.

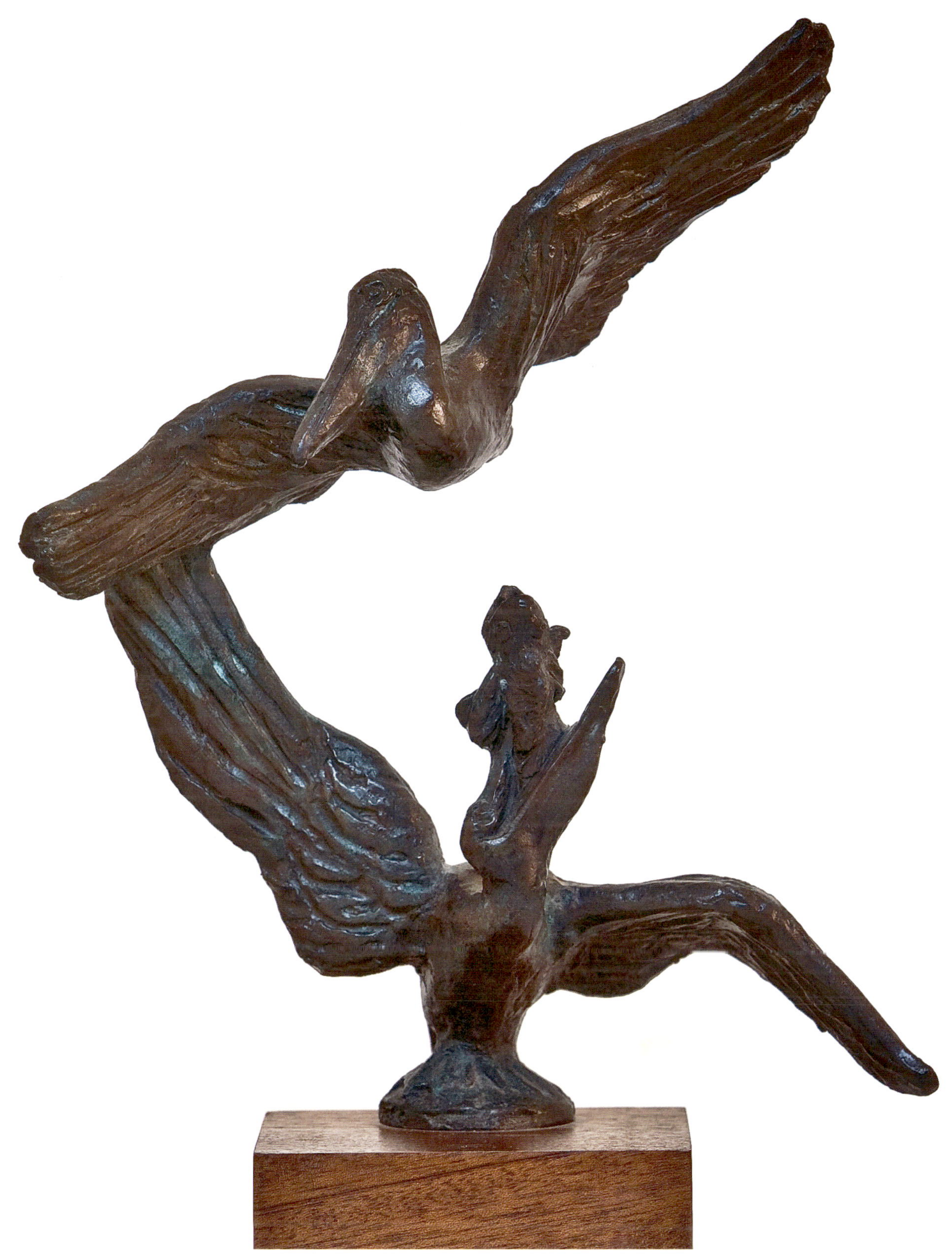

Fig. 52. Willard Hirsch, *Pelicans*, 1982. Bronze, 9 in. tall, Hirsch family collection. Photo by Douglas M. Pinkerton.

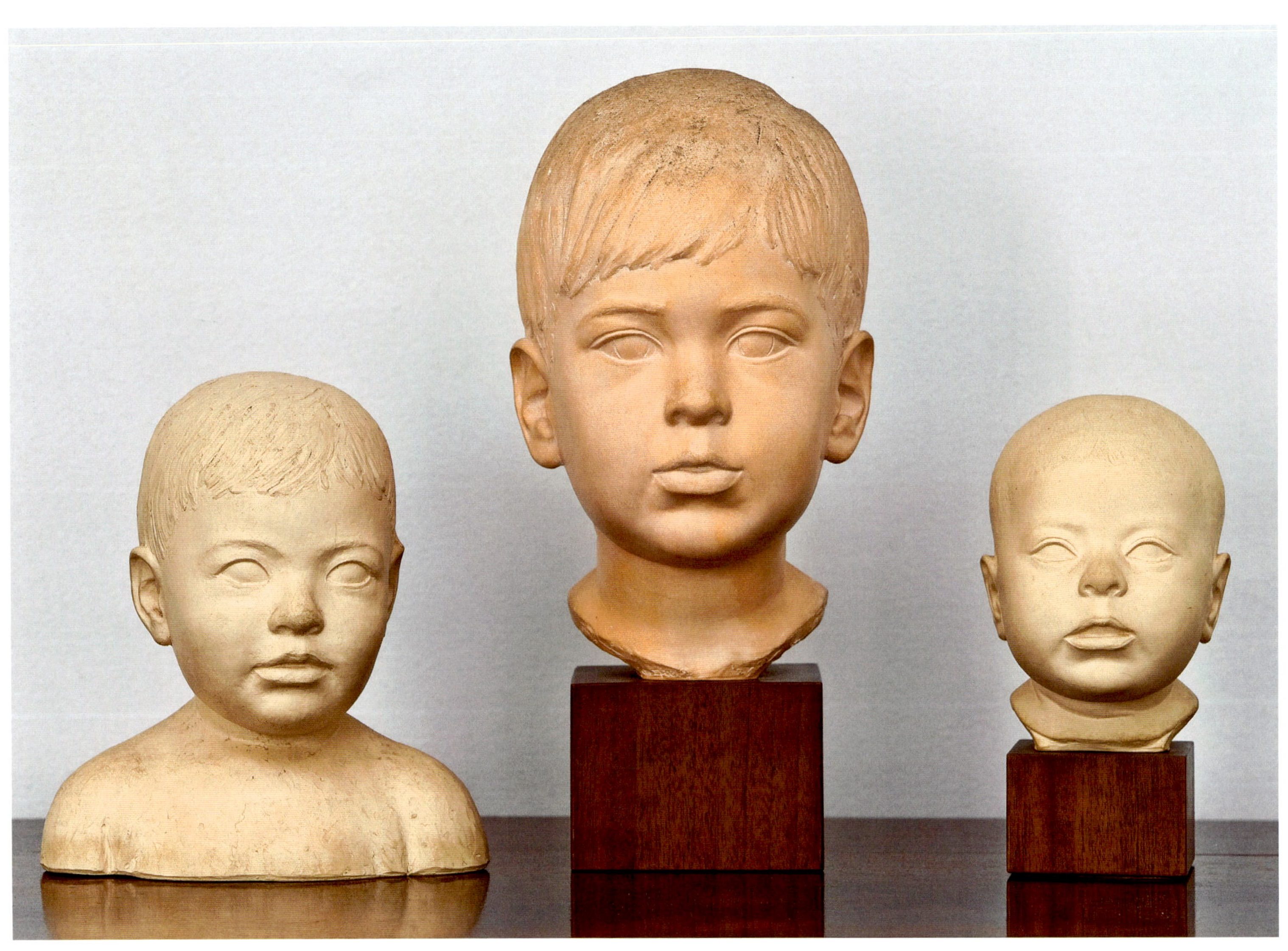

Fig. 53. Willard Hirsch, *Heads of Jack: Six Months,* 1951, terra-cotta, 8 in. tall X 6½ in. wide; *Two Years,* 1953, terra-cotta, 10 in. tall X 6 in. wide; *Six Weeks,* 1951, terra-cotta, 6 in. tall X 3½ in. wide; all Hirsch family collection. Photo by Douglas M. Pinkerton.

Collecting

Jacob Alexander Hirsch

Most of the time, we went collecting either in fresh-water rivers—like the upper Ashley, the Combahee, at Goose Creek, or the Santee—or in saltwater at various locations around Sullivan's Island. The freshwater excursions were big events for me—including eager anticipation, early-morning departures, packed lunches and drinks, and a planned itinerary. There were usually a few specific species we particularly sought, and their habitats determined our itinerary. I was never disappointed about the "success" of our collecting trips—I went for the adventure and the time with Dad. He rarely consulted a map but instead went on some innate sense of direction and distant memories on which he never elucidated. Sometimes we had to ask directions, but only as a last resort. Dad figured if you couldn't find a river, you didn't deserve to fish it.

Fig. 54. Willard Hirsch, *Fish*, 1930s. Terra-cotta, 7 in. tall X 15 in. wide, private collection. Photo by George Frederick Thorpe.

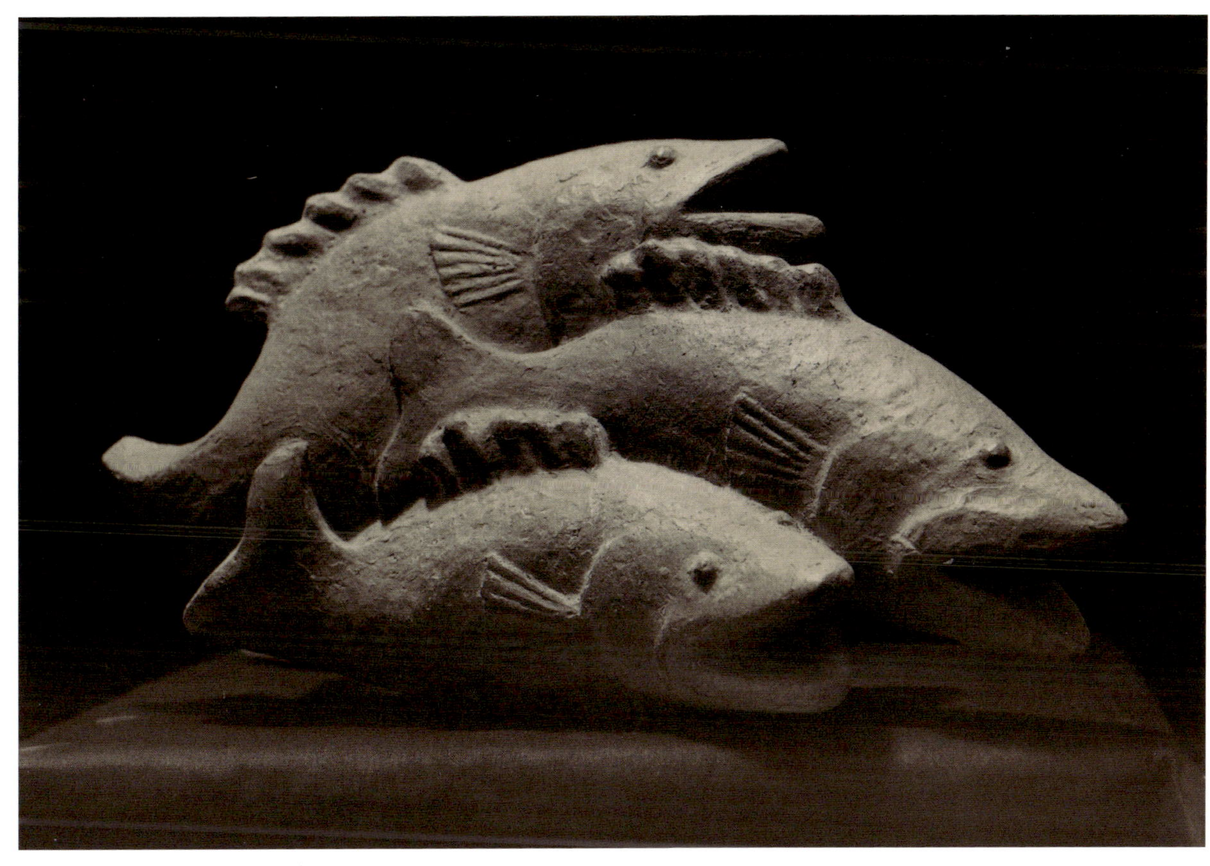

We typically drove on a road along the river, until, for some reason that was always mysterious to me, he would choose a spot to pull over. Then we jumped out to dip up whatever fish might be lurking in the plants by the bank. I generally carried the bucket, although sometimes he let me hold the net and dip—never the first dip, though!

I always worried about snakes and ticks and

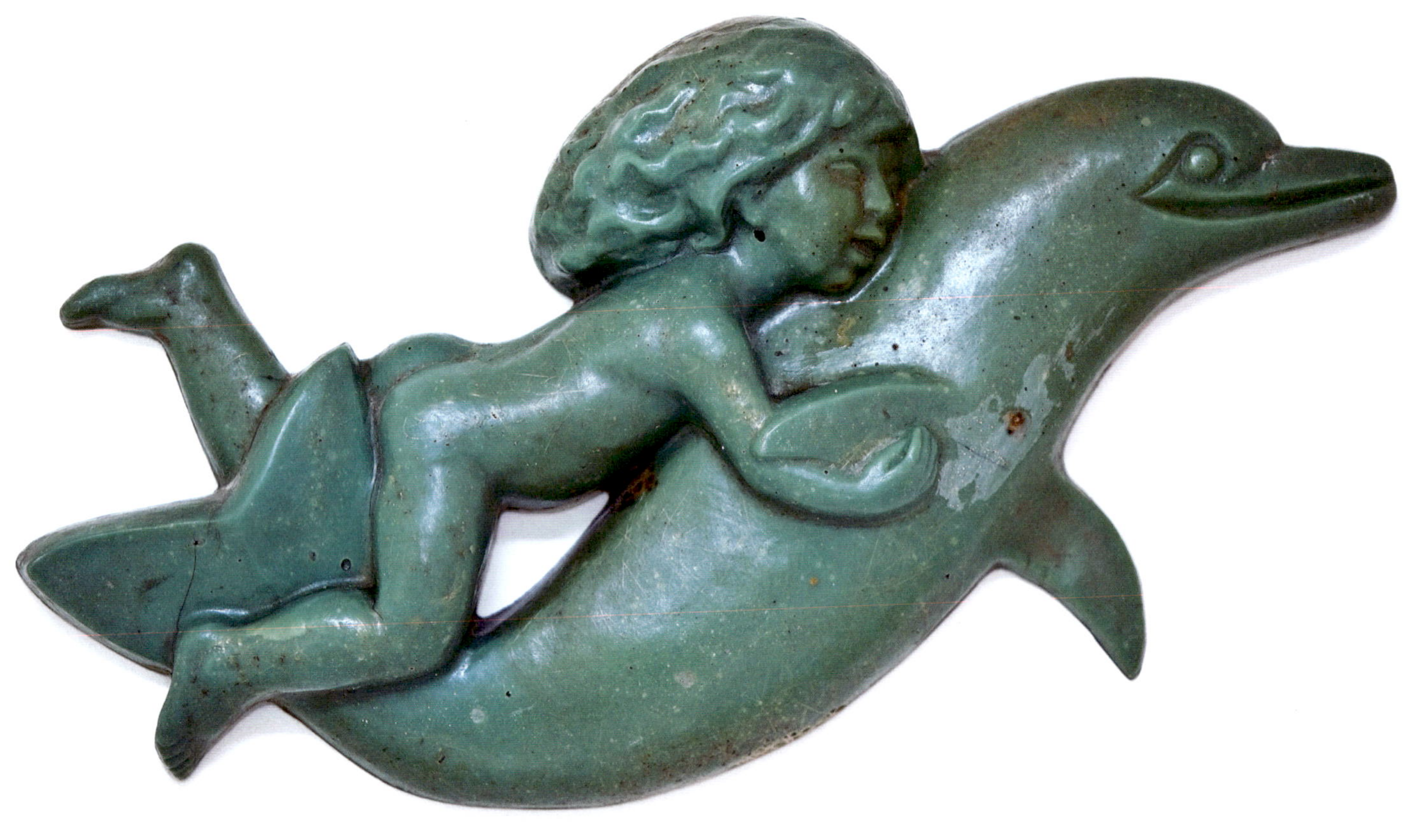

Fig. 55. Willard Hirsch, *Child Riding Porpoise*, n.d. Fiberglass, 8½ in. tall X 16 in. wide, Hirsch family collection. Photo by Douglas M. Pinkerton.

leeches, which was a good thing, because those thoughts took my mind off the mosquitoes and biting flies. The fact was that calling most of these collecting places "rivers" was glorifying them: "swamp" or perhaps "drainage ditch" would have been more accurate. Often these ditches went under roads, so we had to explore both sides. More than a few times, we were surprised by animals hiding in the darkness under the road. They darted away into the dense brush, and, as I typically followed Dad, all I saw was the moving shrubbery. He let me know it was only a fox or raccoon, never a snake!

If the swamp was large enough, or the collecting rewarding enough, we might spend an hour or so dipping into the water. Inevitably, passing motorists pulled over and watched. They often asked, "Need help?" Dad responded, "No."

"Looking for gators?" "No."

"See any moccasins? They're out there, y'know." This made me nervous, but again Dad did not give out any information. His concentration was always fixed on seeing what small fish might be in the water, darting around the plant leaves.

"What'cha catchin'?" Finally, he looked up and said, "Aquarium specimen, if we're lucky."

"Around here?" Dad was not known for patience, and this last comment tipped him over the edge. "If you don't scare them away," he always replied. At that point they usually left in a huff, shaking their heads at our messy task, stumbling around the edges of the smelly swamp.

After several such interruptions, he merely said, "Don't disturb the fish. Just leave us alone," which embarrassed me to no end. "What a nosey busy-body," he added. "Thank goodness they left."

Our saltwater excursions were more fun. The surroundings were usually more pleasant, and we often used a seine, which required a cooperative effort from both of us. Many outings included some surf casting or rock fishing, which I enjoyed. A number of times, we took our Boston Terrier, Teddy, with us, who sniffed around and barked at the waves.

There was one particular time when we were surf fishing, the dog was barking at the waves, and I went out chest deep to heave a mighty cast. I floated around in the water, until suddenly Dad shouted at me to come in. I stumbled in, keeping my line out as far as possible—after all, we were fishing! When I got to Dad, he said, "Someone just rode by on a horse, and Teddy ran after them. Go get him!" So, as an obedient thirteen year-old, I blindly ran after the dog who was chasing after the horse. Yelling was not effective, but neither was my running, as I saw them getting smaller and smaller in the distance. I kept up as long as I could, or perhaps until I realized the futility, and then turned back. I had failed my assignment and lost my dog, and I was afraid that Dad would yell at me. Instead, he had already packed up the fishing gear and said in a rather short-tempered way, "What took so long? Get in the car so we can go get him." Tired, I happily sank into the car seat, and we drove down to the end of the island to find an equally tired dog, who just as happily jumped into the car.

There was one story that Dad loved to recall. Back in those days, he kept a few large saltwater aquariums, which was a very challenging hobby. "Instant Ocean" had not been developed yet, so we had to haul saltwater from the ocean to keep the fish in fresh, clean water. We did this bucket by bucket, so parking close to the water was very important. The best place to do this was Breach Inlet, between Sullivan's Island and the Isle of Palms, where the fast-flowing currents kept the water clean, and one could park only a few hundred yards from the shore. Dad had an old Oldsmobile with a deep trunk that held two fifty-gallon plastic garbage cans upright, only barely visible above the car body. Dad and I used five-gallon buckets, two each, to haul the water to the car and then pour it into the plastic cans. You can imagine the looks people gave us as we made trip after trip pouring saltwater seemingly into the car trunk! Often they made humorous or sarcastic comments. Dad claimed one young family was sunning on the beach as we made trip after trip. Finally, the young girl asked her father, "Daddy, are those men going to empty the ocean?" The father replied, "No, honey. They are just filling up their car!"

When Dad met my future wife, Amy Auslander, he was thrilled to learn she was from Great Neck, New York. As a punster, he was in heaven asking if she was a "great necker?" Did all the girls from her hometown have such long necks? Was necking a high school sport?

Along with puns, Dad was a lover of off-color jokes. I think that the point at which he began telling me his jokes was a reflection of his accepting me as a man, if not an adult. I remember him coming home one evening in a foul mood. I asked what the problem was, and he said he learned an expensive lesson. "When you are driving down the street and see a pretty girl," he said, "always stop, then look." I asked, "Why?" He said, "Because I didn't, and the guy in front of me did!"

When I went to college, Dad seemed to recognize that I was beyond his reach and was making my own decisions. We fought over appearance—he didn't like my beard or long hair—but he seemed to recognize my independence. He was interested in my courses and made suggestions about what to take. He wanted to know what kind of chemistry went on with clays and plaster of Paris. After I was married and had moved back to Charleston, Mom and Dad both were completely understanding and respectful of the privacy my wife and I wanted while we lived there for six years.

Jacob Alexander Hirsch lives in Amherst, Massachusetts, where he is a chemist at the University of Massachusetts. He and his wife, Amy, have two sons, Phillip and Alexander. Jack still enjoys keeping aquariums.

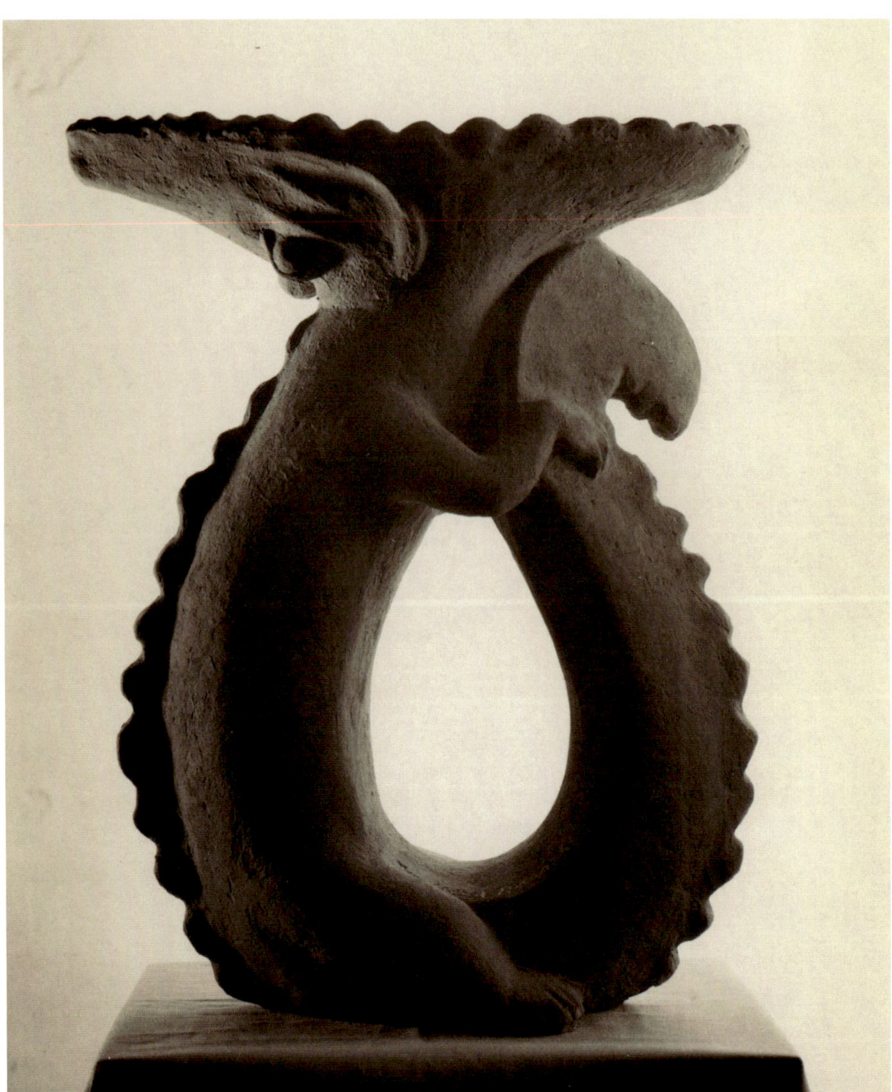

Fig. 56. Willard Hirsch, Alligator birdbath, n.d. Terra-cotta, 21 in. tall, private collection. Photo by George Frederick Thorpe.

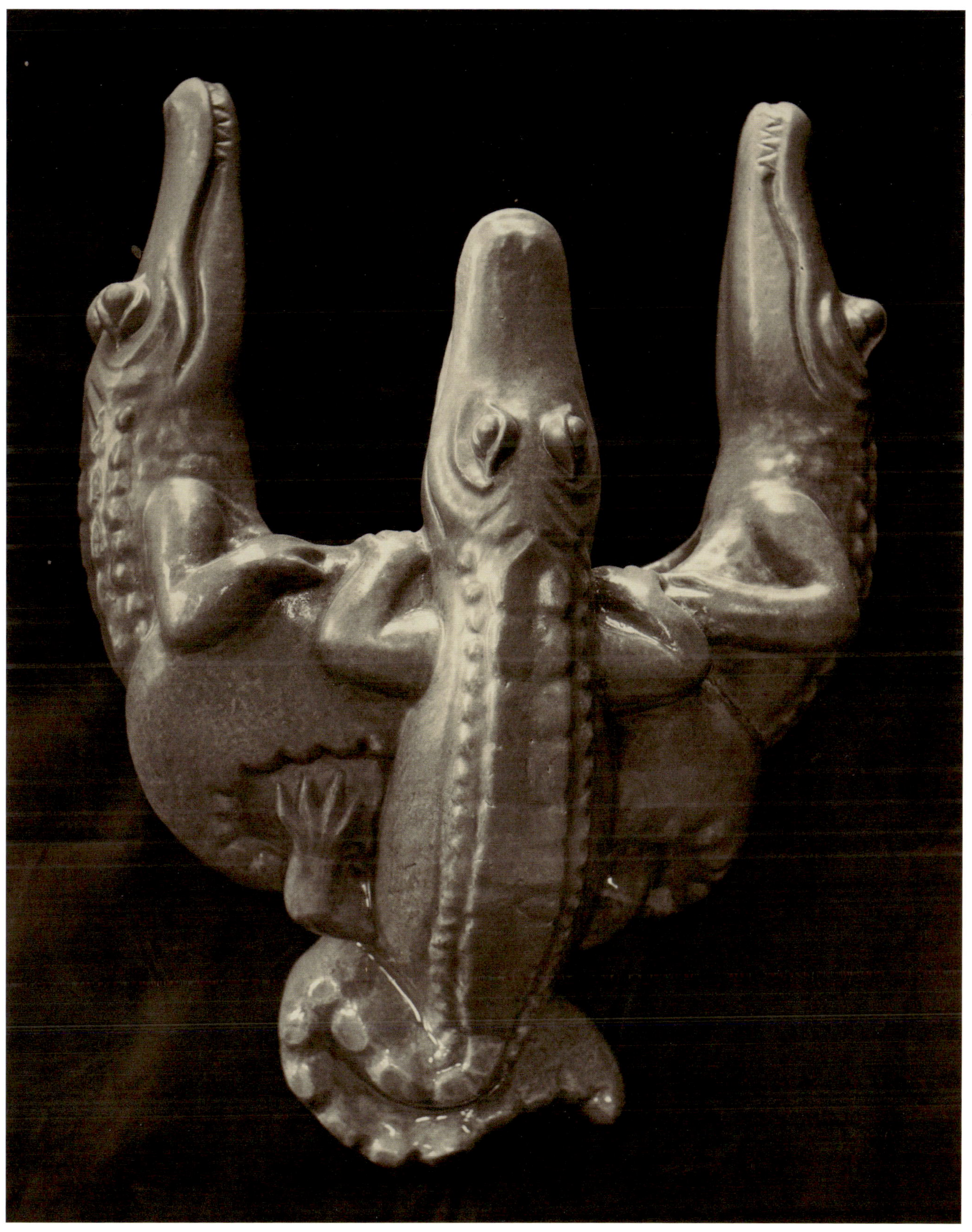

Fig. 57. Willard Hirsch, Alligator wall fountain, n.d. Terra-cotta, 23 in. tall, private collection. Hirsch family collection.

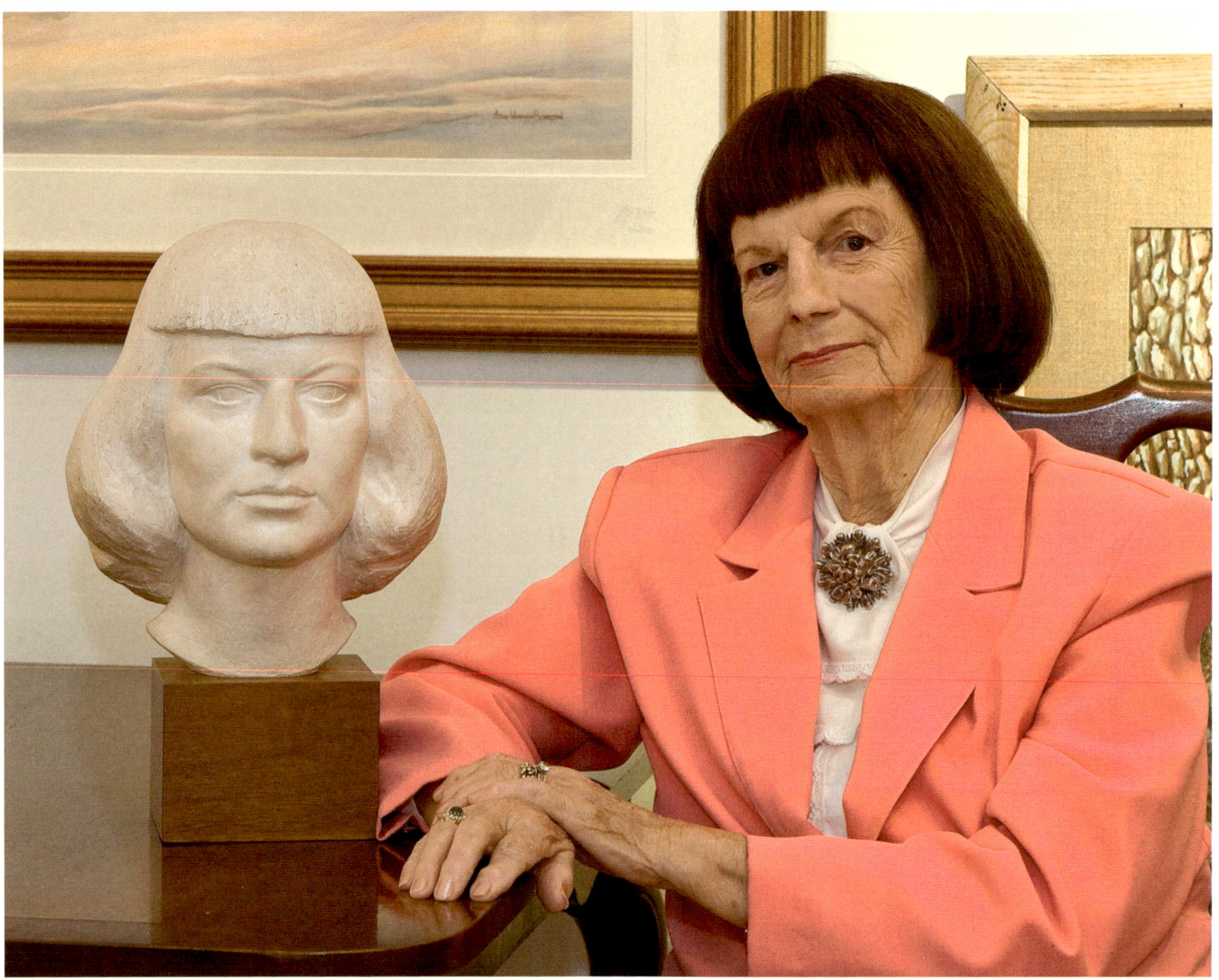

Fig. 58. Anne Worsham Richardson with her sculptured head by Willard Hirsch. Photo by Douglas M. Pinkerton.

One Head for Two Little Owls

By Anne Worsham Richardson

When we met in 1953 Willard Hirsch was the most striking and charming artist I had ever known. That year we were both founders of the Charleston Artist Guild.

In 1959 he invited me to share a joint exhibition at Emmett Johnson's gallery at 23 Queen Street. It was to be the first time that I had an exhibition in Charleston, though I had exhibited in the Kennedy Gallery in New York in 1958 and in Macon, Georgia, and North Carolina. I was honored and excited about my first Charleston exhibition with such an accomplished artist.

About a month before it was to take place, Willard was demonstrating how to do a portrait for the Charleston Artist Guild at the Gibbes Art Gallery. To my surprise, he chose me out of the crowd to be the model. As I took my place up front for this special honor, I laughed and said, "I know why you selected me. I have bangs and a big nose, so you can get a likeness right away!"

It was interesting to see his gifted hands shape the clay into my face and head. After the meeting, he asked me if I could come by his studio and let him complete the details. I agreed, and soon he had my portrait finished, and it was just like me! I asked if my portrait would be in our forthcoming exhibit, and he answered, "No, your head is too big!"

When our showing opened and the guests arrived, I saw that one of the sculptures was covered with a white veil. Willard went over and unveiled the portrait of me with a flourish and spotlighted my work. He was so generous to make such a grand gesture.

After our exhibit was over and we had packed our work to take home, I saw that he had not packed my portrait. "Aren't you going to pack my head?" I asked. Willard said, "No. I think you can use another head." I offered to pay him but he refused. Instead, he said that he would like my painting, *Two Little Owls on a Pine Limb*. So we made the exchange with fun—one head for two little owls! *(Figure 53)*

I was young then and he often teased me. At an exhibition of fifty of my "Birds of America" paintings at the Gibbes in 1965, Willard looked over my work and commented, "Anne, why do you, such a calm, peaceful person, often paint birds fighting?" I explained, "Willard, they aren't fighting. That is a part of their courtship display." He replied, "Same thing!"

Willard had a great exhibition at the Gibbes, which my husband John Peter Paszek attended with me. John saw a beautiful bronze of *The Little Dancer* and he bought it for me. It is such a treasure, and when I look at it I recall many happy memories of our years of friendship. It was an honor to call him and his beautiful wife, Mordenai, and their two children, Jane and Jack, my friends.

Anne Worsham Richardson is a nationally and internationally known painter who still paints and maintains her Birds I View Gallery on Church Street.

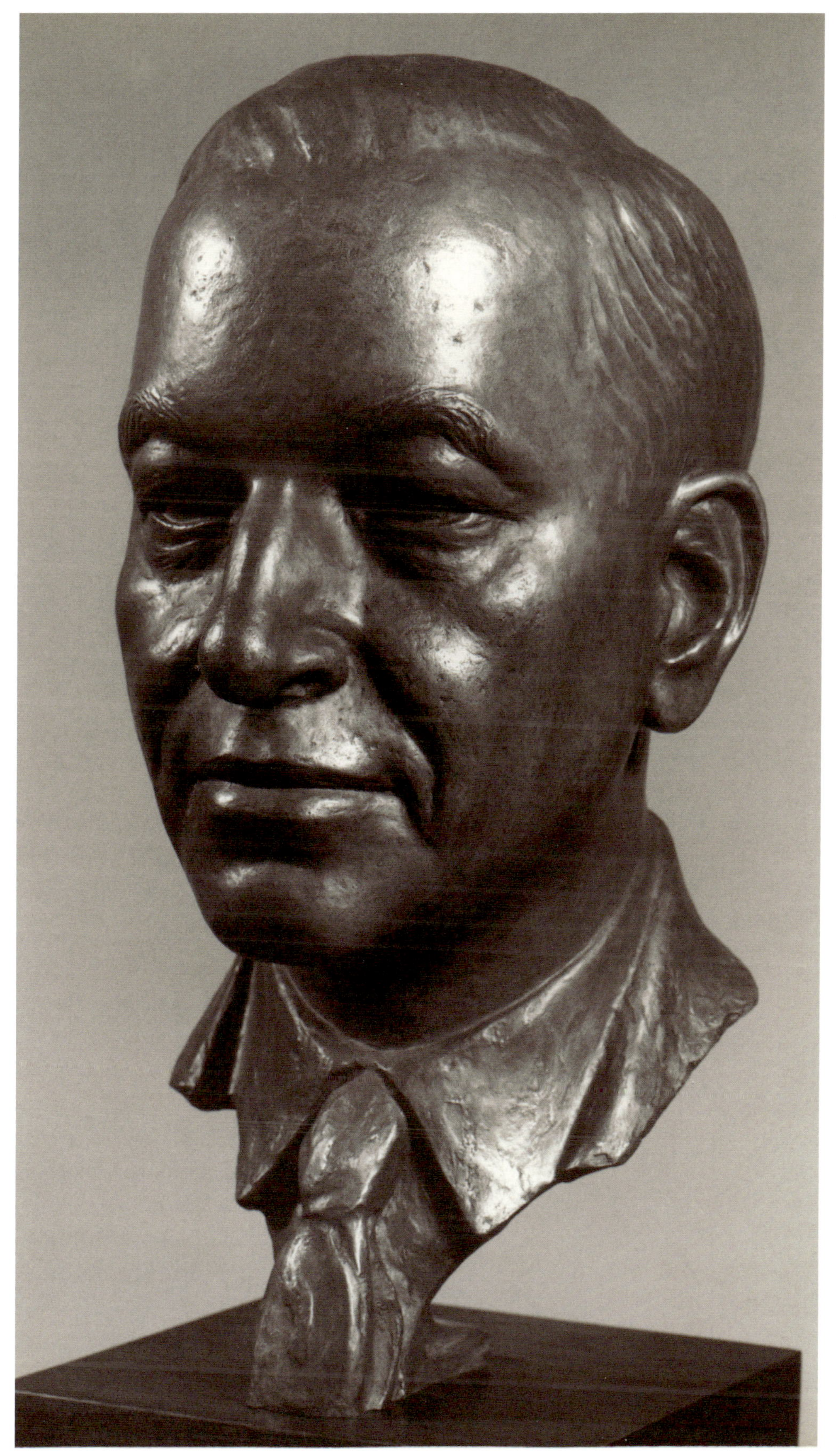

Fig. 59. Willard Hirsch, *Robert McCormick Figg* (dean of USC School of Law), n.d. Bronze, private collection. Photo by Louis Schwartz.

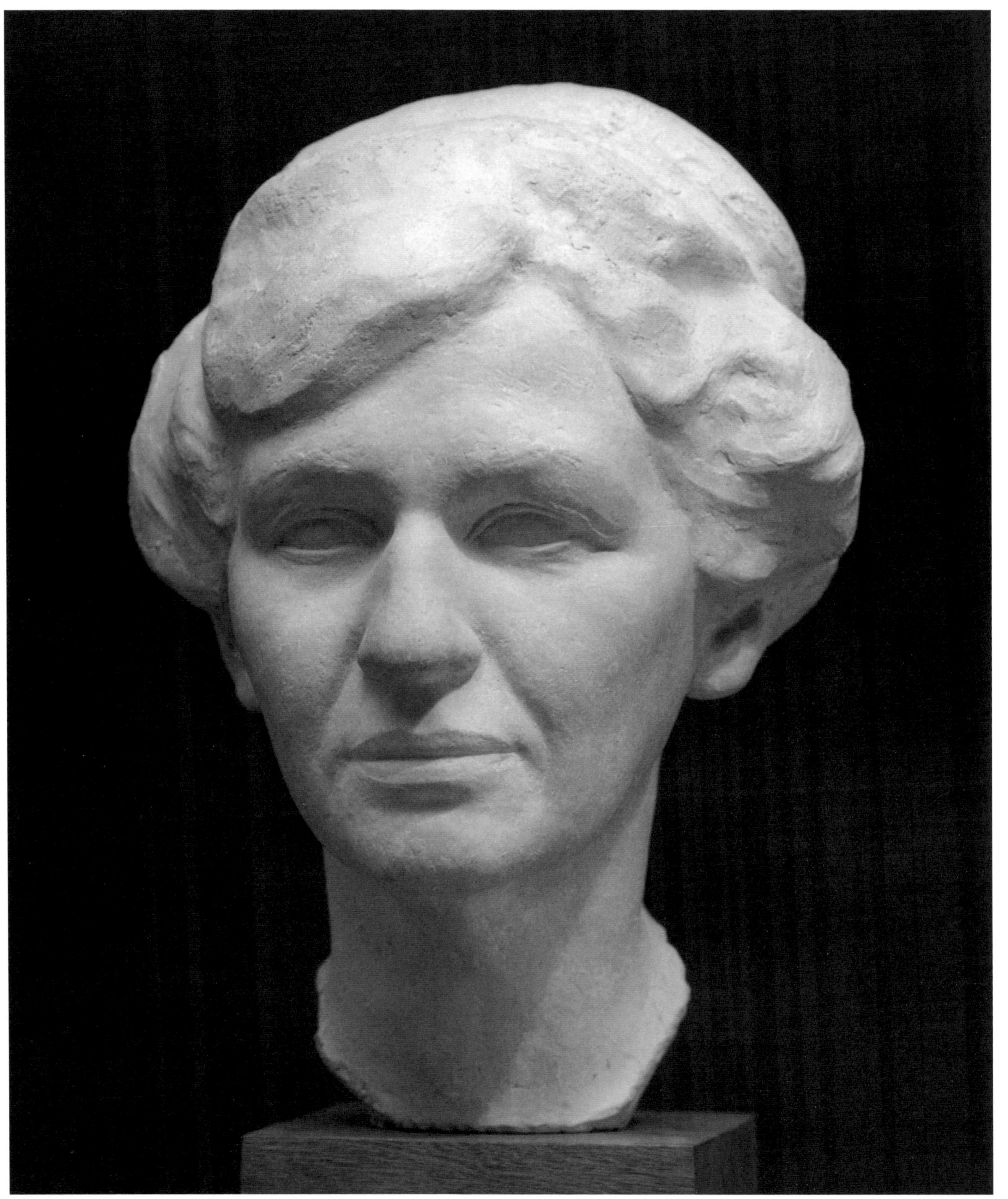

Fig. 60. Willard Hirsch, *Laura Bragg,* 1969. Terra-cotta, 13 in. tall X 10 in. wide X 9 in. deep, Gibbes Museum of Art, Charleston, S.C. Photo by Louis Schwartz.

"Make It Yourself"

By Katherine Muschick Schneider

I had the privilege of working for Mr. Hirsch as his studio assistant from 1979 to 1981. Most of the notes I took were about his sculpture methods and materials: armature making, sculpting in kaolin clay and plasticine, making piece molds for plaster and clay casting, working with foundries for metal and bronze casting, creating bas-relief sculptures, and mounting finished work, as well as maintaining studio records and practices.

I remember a piece of advice he gave me: "Never stop until you've done the best you can. But then again, leave well enough alone."

One day in the studio, while we were working on a portrait of a child, I asked Mr. Hirsch if he had ever done a self-portrait. He replied that Miss Laura Bragg *(Figure 60)* had asked him the same question, to which he replied that he was too cheap to pay himself the price for doing a portrait. She told him that his prices must be too high!

At one point, we were discussing difficulties I was having with a portrait bust of my mother. Mr. Hirsch said it had taken him over a year to complete his first bas-relief of his mother. I was having trouble sculpting her eyes, because I didn't have the right tool for the task. He said that Mr. Robert Aitken, one of his teachers at the National Academy of Design in New York, told a fellow student, "If you don't have a tool you need, make it yourself." He then helped me improvise a tool out of a paper clip. Having lived through the Great Depression and being frugal, he re-bent the paper clip after I had finished using it and put it back into the drawer!

Katherine Muschick Schneider is a working artist in Charleston. She maintains an art blog, http://paintcharlestondaily.blogspot.com, on which she has written several times about Hirsch.

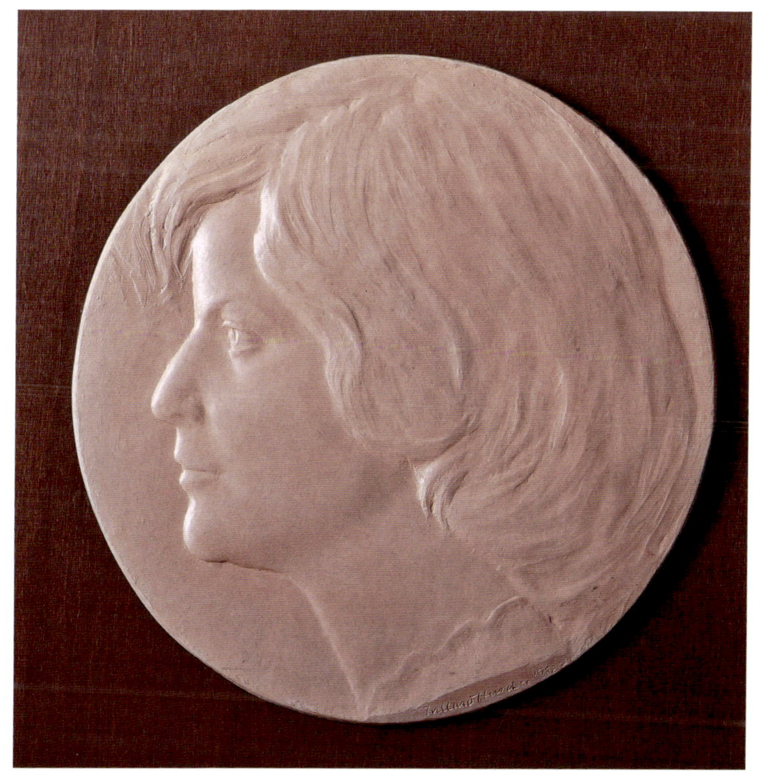

Fig. 61. Willard Hirsch, *Katherine Muschick Schneider,* 1982. Terra-cotta, 11¼ in. X 11¼ in., private collection. Photo by Douglas M. Pinkerton.

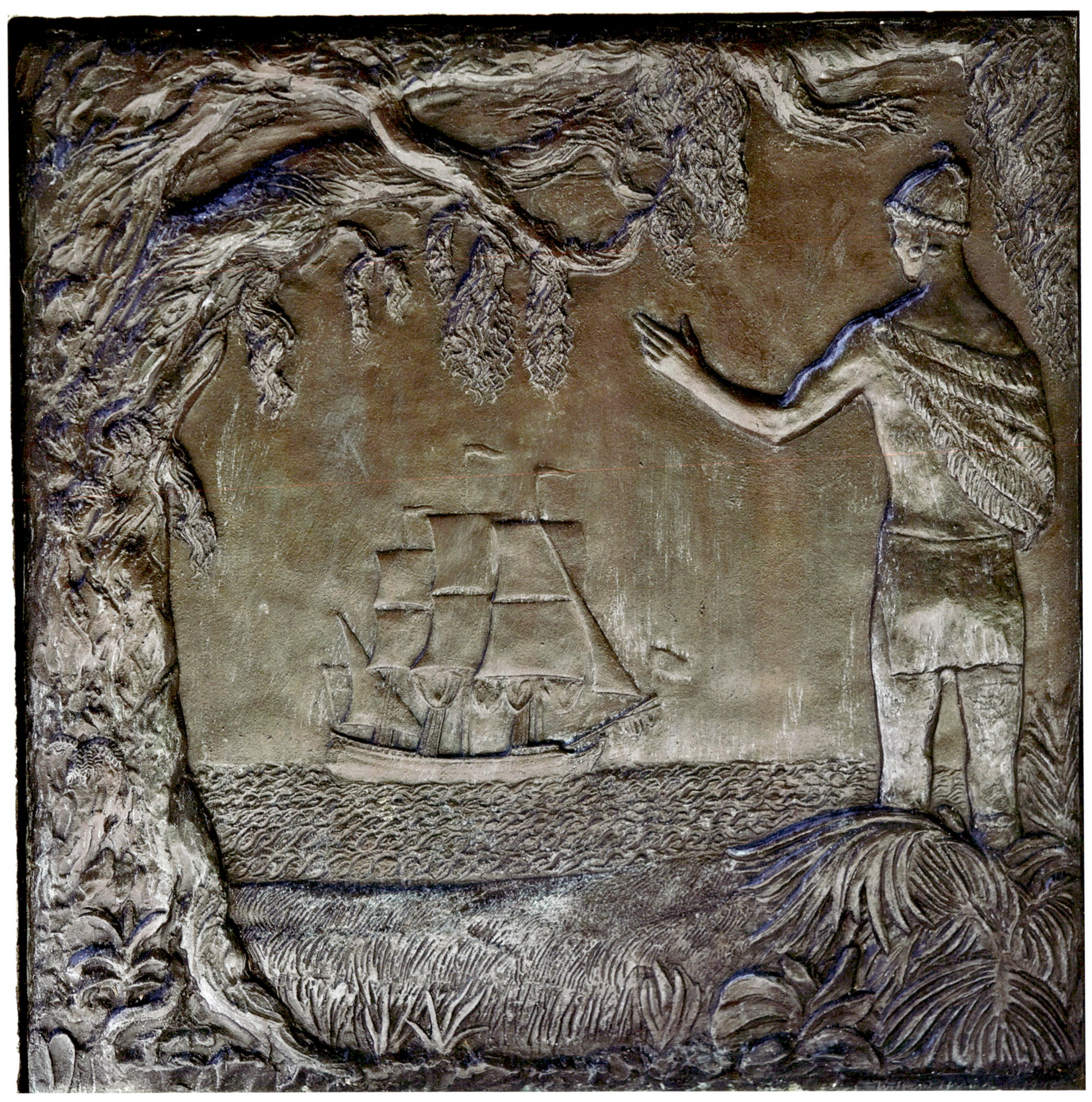

Fig. 63. Willard Hirsch, base of *Cassique of Kiawah*, 1971-72. Bronze, 24 in. tall X 24 in. wide, Charles Towne Landing, Charleston, S.C. Photo by Douglas M. Pinkerton.

Fairy Tales

By Thomas E. Thornhill

Fig. 63. Willard Hirsch, Model for *Cassique of Kiawah*, 1970. Plaster, 26 in. tall, Hirsch family collection. Photo by Douglas M. Pinkerton.

I knew Willard Hirsch most of my adult life, but it was during the state's Tricentennial celebration, 1969-1972, that we got to be good friends. I was chairman of the Charleston County Tricenntennial Committee and a member of the state commission. The South Carolina Tricentennial Commission purchased Old Town plantation, the site of the landing of the first permanent settlement, from Mrs. Joseph Waring to make the state park Charles Towne Landing. The original landing took place in April 1670, so the celebration was focused on April 1970. We wanted to commission a statue of the Cassique of the Kiawah Indians who directed the settlers to the site of Charles Towne. *The State* advertised for submissions, and, as I remember, Willard and one other submitted sketches. There was a judging panel and Willard was selected. So for months, I visited his studio to view the progress until the model *(Figure 63)*, which was four feet or so high, was sent to the foundry to be cast into the eight-and-a-half-foot statue that now stands at the Charles Towne Landing State Historic Site. Also, during that time, he was doing a number of head sculptures. I believe one was of his daughter Jane, and another of Mayor Palmer Gaillard, which now stands at Gaillard Auditorium.

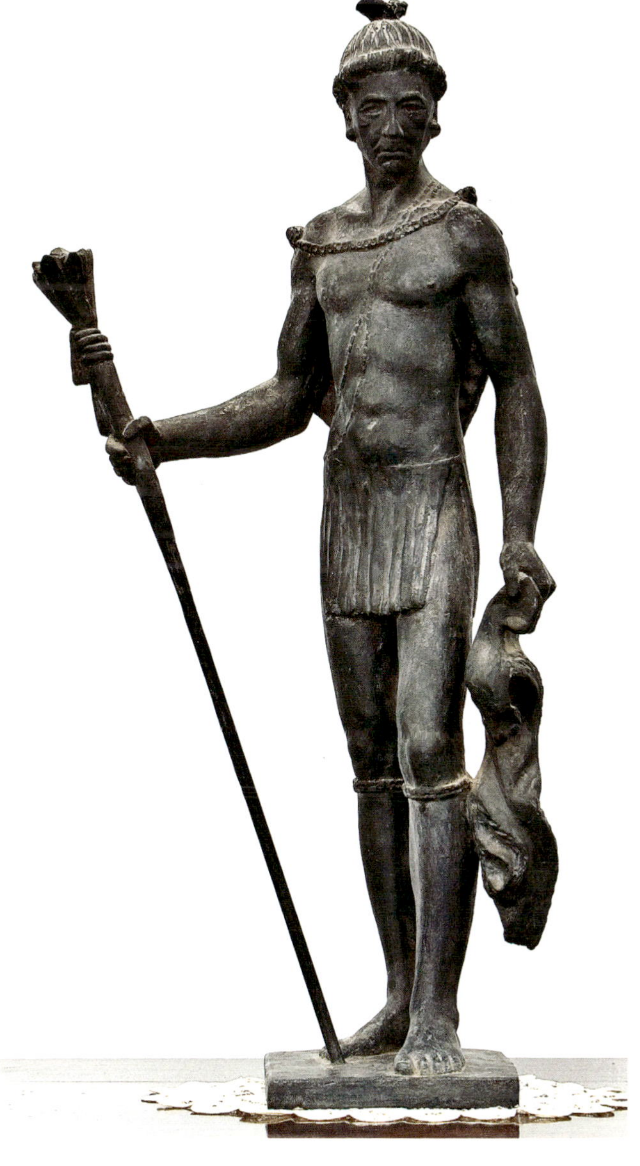

During these visits to his studio, we would talk about politics, the town, and some religion. He was very opinionated and stuck to his theories, but that was part of the fun, to pick at him sometimes about his stance on something. One time, I mentioned something about Jesus Christ, and he went into a tirade of how that was all a fairy tale made up by some disgruntled Jews. I retorted with the idea that it was the same people who made up the story of Moses, Jeremiah, Isaac, and all the rest. He just grinned at me, and we did not discuss religion anymore.

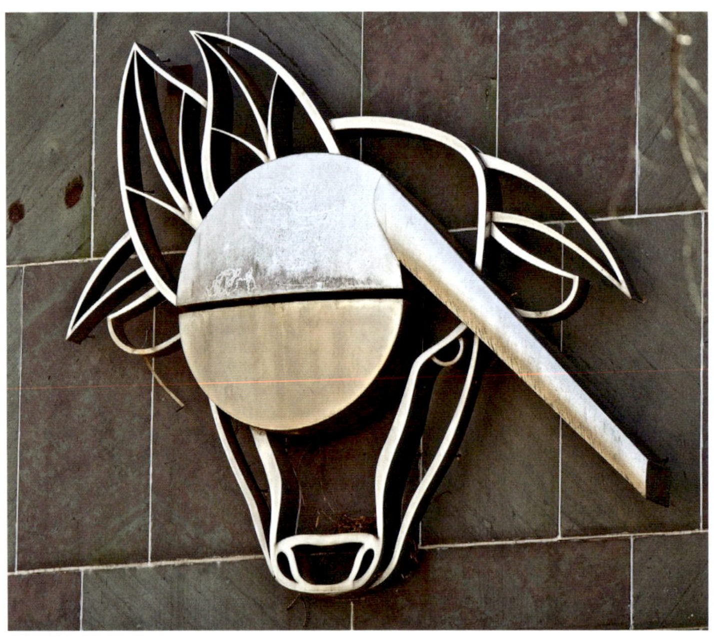

Fig. 64. Willard Hirsch, *Bull and Retort*, 1955. Stainless steel, 7 ft. tall X 8 ft. wide, Plant and Animal Science Building, Clemson University, Clemson, S.C. Photo by Douglas M. Pinkerton.

It was always fascinating to me to see his sketches and learn where his work was—at Clemson *(see Figure 64)*, Newberry *(see Figures 65 and 66)*, all over. He knew I was a devoted Clemson graduate, so we discussed the *Clemson Tiger* and the pieces on the Agriculture Building many times. One of my most treasured possessions is the model for the *Tiger*. When he was closing his shop, he called me one day and asked me to stop by. I went in to see him and he told me that he had asked that when he died all of his sketches and molds be destroyed, but he wanted me to have the *Tiger*. What a wonderful gesture! It is a two-foot stainless-steel model for the seven-foot piece that now graces the front of The Clemson House on the campus. (See *Figure 12)*

Thomas E. (Tommy) Thornhill is a local businessman and community leader. He has served as president of the Charleston Metro Chamber of Commerce, the Historic Charleston Foundation, the Kiwanis Club, and the United Way. He wrote a letter to the Charleston News and Courier *in 1983 asking for contributions to the Willard Hirsch Memorial Fund. This fund bought the* Falling Angel *for the Gibbes Art Gallery, which was installed in front of its school on Queen Street. It is now in the garden behind the Gibbes Museum of Art on Meeting Street.*

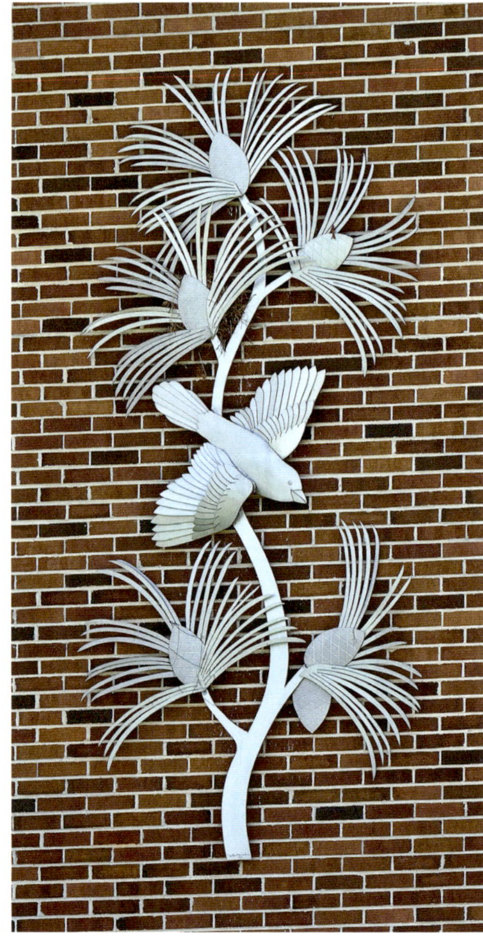

Fig. 65. Willard Hirsch, Bachman Sparrow, 1973. Aluminum, 10 ft. tall, Alumni Music Building, Newberry College, Newberry, S.C. Photo by Douglas M. Pinkerton.

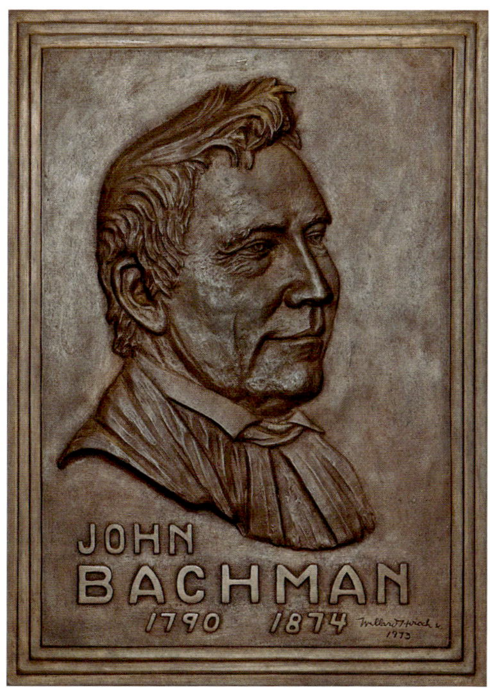

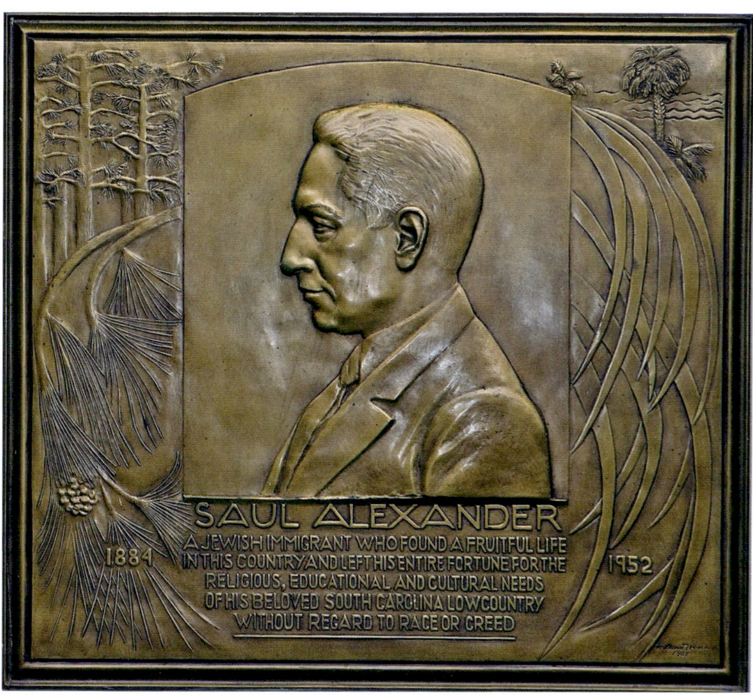

Fig. 66. Willard Hirsch, *Dr. John Bachman* (founder of Newberry College and first chairman of the school's board of trustees), 1974. Bronze, Lenora McClurg Center for Teaching and Learning, Newberry College, Newberry, S.C. Photo by Douglas M. Pinkerton.

Fig. 67. Willard Hirsch, *Saul Alexander*, 1962. Bronze, 29 in. tall X 34 in. wide, Charleston County Public Library, Charleston, S.C. Photo by Douglas M. Pinkerton.

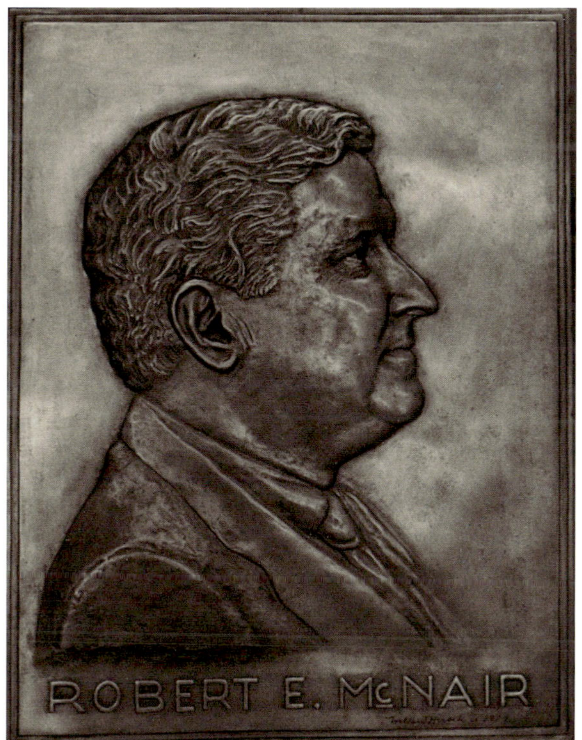

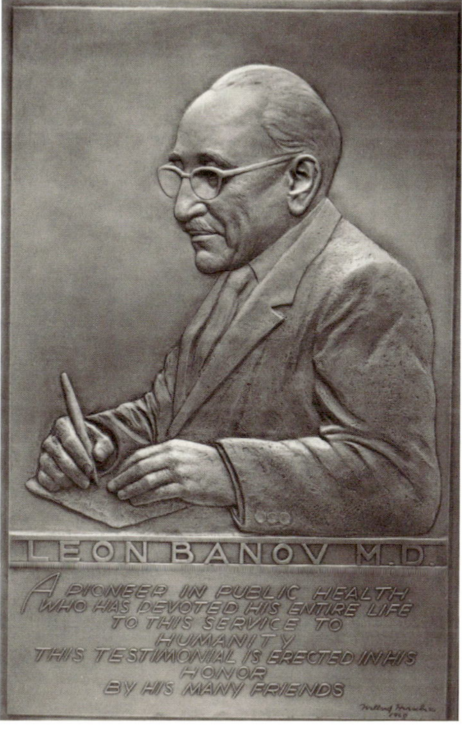

Fig. 68. Willard Hirsch, *Robert E. McNair*, 1974. Bronze, 24½ in. tall X 19 in. wide, McNair Science Building, Francis Marion College, Florence, S.C. Photo by Louis Schwartz.

Fig. 69. Willard Hirsch, *Leon Banov, M.D.*, 1969. Bronze, 36 in. wide X 24 in. tall, Charleston County Health Clinic, Charleston, S.C. Photo by Louis Schwartz.

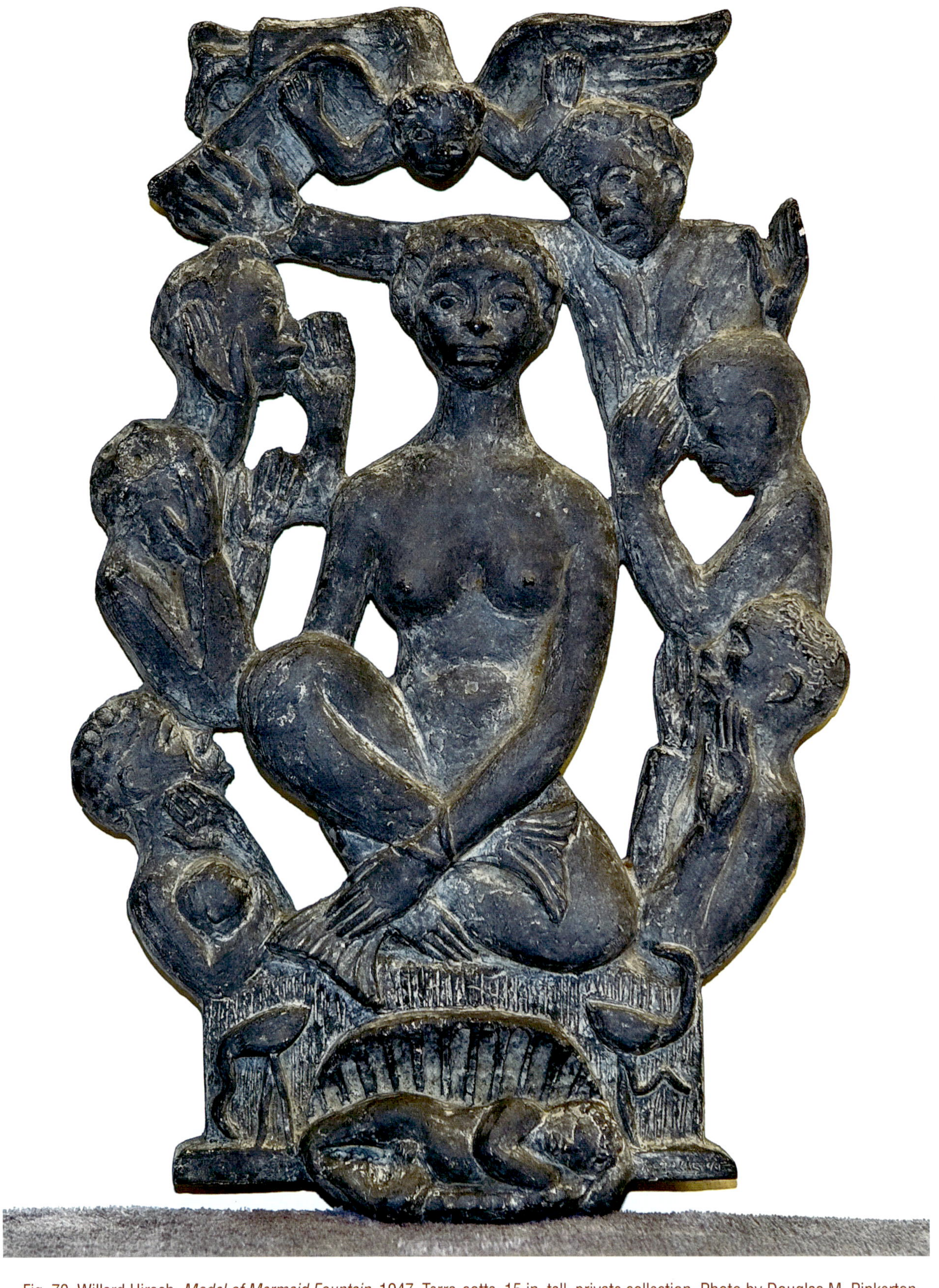

Fig. 70. Willard Hirsch, *Model of Mermaid Fountain*, 1947. Terra-cotta, 15 in. tall, private collection. Photo by Douglas M. Pinkerton.

God and Mr. Hirsch

Harlan Greene

The name "Hirsch" brings on a flood of childhood memories. The Hirsch children were our age, so my siblings and I and the Hirsch kids were in and out of each other's houses, theirs mostly, appealing for its long piazzas, joggling board, sandbox, and a very large cat, Napoleon, aptly nicknamed Nappy. Though I remember Mr. Hirsch in his push-button Morris chair or presiding at meals, his hearing aid attuning him to a different world from mine, his real domain was elsewhere. Recently, that world of his literally came back to me in the shape of a clay figurine I had given to a friend about fifty years ago, a figure that had started its "life" in Mr. Hirsch's studio on Exchange Street. That was the universe where he ruled.

My mother dropped me off, and waited to make sure I went in. It took all my courage to push the door open and make my way upstairs, sort of like that steep and narrow stairway of *A Chorus Line*. I remember irregular wooden steps and that nervous flutter of anticipation each time I went in. The damp earthy smell of the wet clay was instantaneous, a sort of subterranean cave-like scent, even though the top floor had huge windows and was flooded with light. Memory may not be correct, but I see us, his students, sitting at long tables. Fish in the tanks stared at us expectantly.

A wet ball of clay was plopped on the table. We were twins, that clay and I; I was just as amorphous as it. The command, "Don't just sit there like a lump of clay," was something hurled often at me in my childhood, but Mr. Hirsch would never have said it, for to him nothing was more inspirational. A ball of clay in Willard Hirsch's hands must have triggered the same sensation that God had on the first day of creation. God and Mr. Hirsch could spin universes of beauty out of such humble raw material.

Not me. I eyed the lump suspiciously, and with a bit of fear, knowing that, static as it was, it was probably going to best me.

Mr. Hirsch had to be patient—not his long suit. But children could be taught art, for a small fee, even if their parents would not buy it from the artist.

We began with the lower order of creation—reptiles, I think. Mr. Hirsch showed us how to make a turtle. My memory—not his daughter's—is that forming a ball and then flattening it worked for the shell; you could

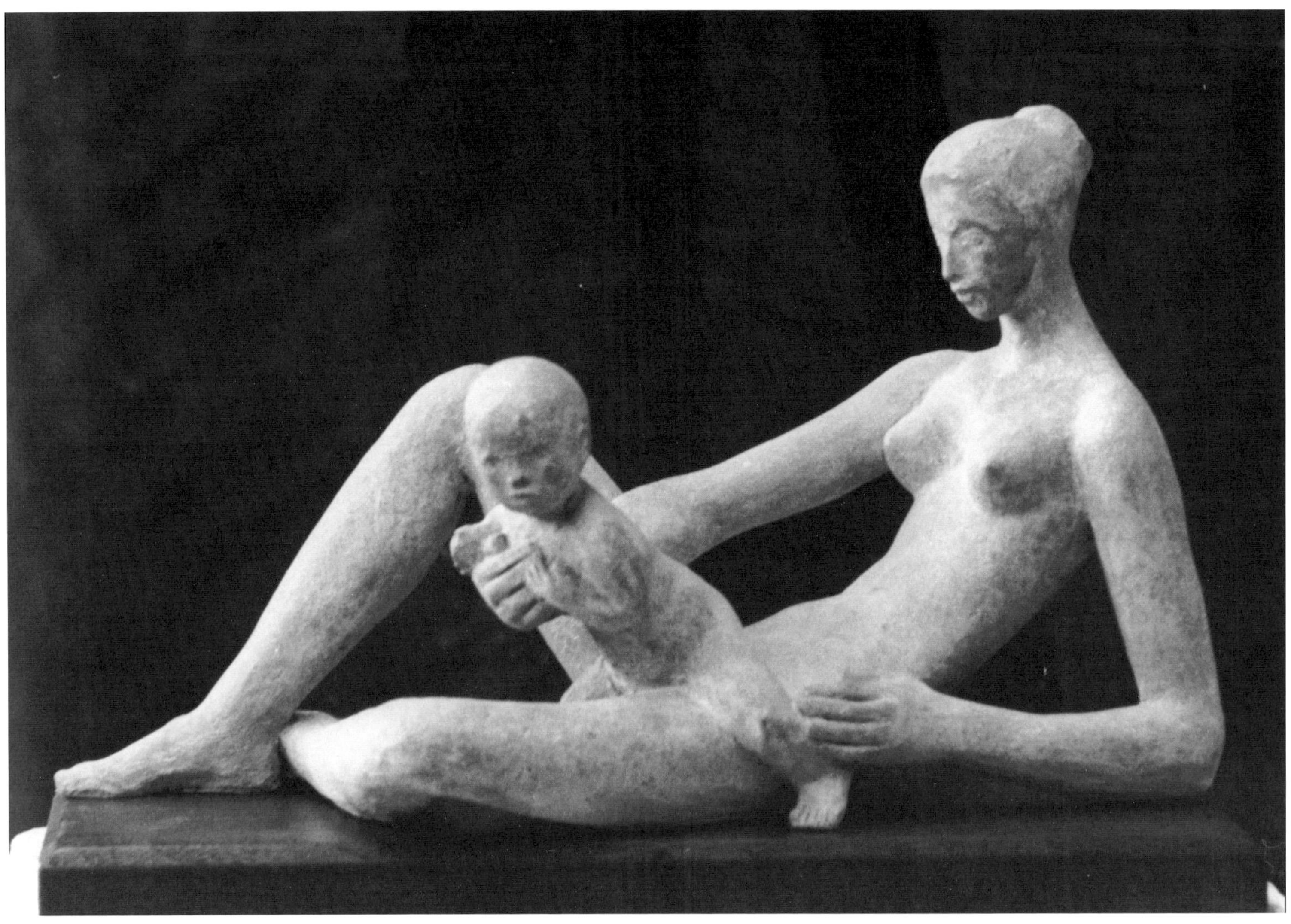

Fig. 71. Willard Hirsch, *Mother and Child,* 1937. Terra-cotta, 8 in. tall X 14 in. long, private collection. Photo by Louis Schwartz.

then roll three thin sausage-shaped tubes—one straight, placed in the middle for the head and tail; then you'd curve one tube on either side of that in "C" formations to be the feet, which would stick out once you attached the shell. That demonstrated, we were on our own.

I wanted to follow rules, but there were precious few in Mr. Hirsch's studio. One could dream fantastic things, of course, but the idea of acting them out or making them real, creating something out of nothing, seemed disobedient and mildly shocking.

So I soldiered on clumsily. The malformed creatures I modeled and that Mr. Hirsch fired constituted an embarrassing parade of the halt and lame that I dutifully took home to show my mother, and she, in turn, made dutiful sounds over them.

One day, the hand of God and Mr. Hirsch descended, and I saw creation in action. I had been working on a tiger, slowly and inexpertly. Mr. Hirsch came along and—disgusted with my clumsiness, wanting my parents to get value for their fees, or maybe in a wave of pity for the tiger—he intervened. With a few deft lines drawn in the wet clay with a tool and pressure from his fingers, my sad beast suddenly came alive!

And when that tiger was fired and finished, I proudly took it home to assume its place in front of the sad menagerie of lopsided creatures. Its head was turned as if looking at me; it had stripes. I could imagine light through thick green foliage, as this bright beast moved stealthily through the jungle, before leaping. Like Blake's Tyger, it burned bright in my mind, along with a bit of guilt that although Mr. Hirsch had written my name on it, it was more his creation than mine.

I'm sure many Charlestonians my age harbor the same guilty secret: it was not the artist in me that did that, but the artist who lived down the street. He opened the door to beauty and let me believe I had a chance at creativity; much later and after the fact, the message came to me.

I see now what I could not as a kid: Willard Hirsch was not afraid to put in words what he thought, or to put into three dimensions the beauty and transcendence and whimsy he found in the world. Belatedly, as most wisdom comes, I saw there had been a role model for me down the street.

Maybe to repay Mr. Hirsch for his struggles with her awkward son, my mother bought a few of his finished pieces. Each time I chanced to come upon our bronze of *Joy of Motherhood*, or the terra-cotta piece *Mother and Child (Figure 71)*, I was held by their joy of line, of life, of human creation and creativity. And years later when Mrs. Hirsch and Jane presented me with a "doodle" of his plan for a fountain based on the Charleston mermaid folktale (if a mermaid is held captive, rain will fall until she can return to her child in the sea} *(Figure 70)*, it went up on my wall immediately.

I'm greedy. I love beauty. So when an old childhood friend told me she had one of the clay figures I had made in Mr. Hirsch's studio, I grew excited. My still-clumsy hands had a hard time opening the box and undoing the wrapping. I knew it would be the tiger and that I'd have another beautiful Willard Hirsch piece. But no, it was a sad little sheep—or dog. I'm not sure what it is exactly, some mutant thing with a body, legs, a face, and ears. That sad creature went back into its box, where it lies dormant, sending out pulses of memory.

When I take it out, I imagine instead the tiger that Mr. Hirsch and I made together in that transcendent act we shared for an instant. I see that, imperfect as are my current pieces (literary not sculptural), I can still nevertheless try to add my paltry contribution to the universe, a lesson learned first in Mr. Hirsch's studio on the aptly named Exchange Street. For something was exchanged and changed back there: me. More than statues, Mr. Hirsch was molding and firing a whole generation of Charleston children in his studio. I can imagine the impact he had on countless embryonic artists and appreciators of beauty, knowing what he did for a lump of clay like me.

Harlan Greene, author and archivist, grew up down the street from Willard Hirsch.

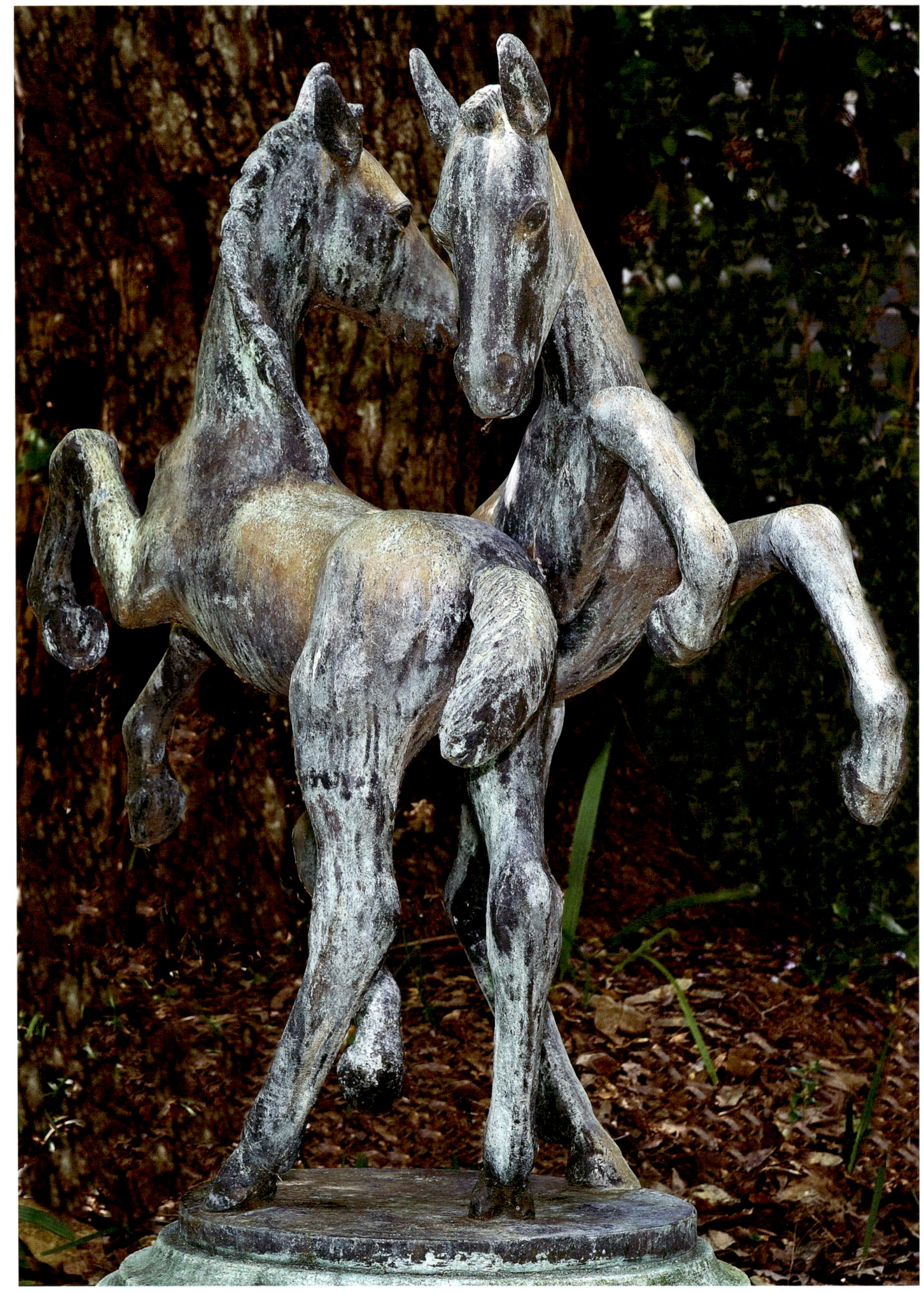

Fig. 72. Willard Hirsch, *Prancing Colts*, 1956. Bronze, 43 in. tall, private collection. Photo by Douglas M. Pinkerton.

"No Ashtrays!"

By Joseph Harrison

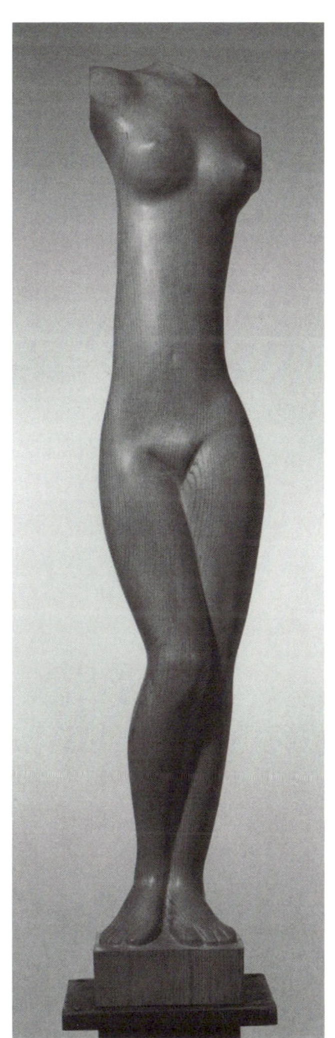

Fig. 73. Willard Hirsch, *Torso*, n.d. Spruce, 41in. tall, locaton unknown.

In the late 1950s I was fortunate to attend the Gaud School for Boys when the headmaster believed in the value of including the arts in the curriculum. The three most notable Charleston artists at that time, Corrie McCallum and William Halsey for painting and Willard Hirsch for sculpture, were employed to give us an hour of studio instruction each week. I was partial to sculpture, and to the dynamic personality and teaching style of Mr. Hirsch. So began my encounter, in the ninth grade if memory serves, with Willard Hirsch, a superb professional sculptor and gifted teacher.

Our studio was on a second floor in a building near Adger's Wharf. There was a long narrow staircase leading up, and when I hit the bottom stair and could detect the distinctive smell of the clay, I knew the hour would be interesting and instructive—in short, fun. Mr. Hirsch's teaching style combined humor, short poems, and practiced hands-on instruction. He possessed a fine sense of sequence and was able to lead each student from the simplest instruction to ever-greater complexity. I discovered that you could make a turtle by fashioning an ice cream cone (tail and head), two hotdogs (legs), and a hamburger (shell). Simply attach the two hot dogs to the central cone and then place the hamburger on top and press down. Suddenly, a turtle emerged!

If you progressed a little bit, you got into anatomy. Willard Hirsch was expert in the anatomy of all kinds of animals *(Figure 72)* and, of course, of human beings. *(Figures 73* and *74)* He knew proportions and where muscles should swell or recede. His eye for these things was unerring. I did not learn about the trapezius

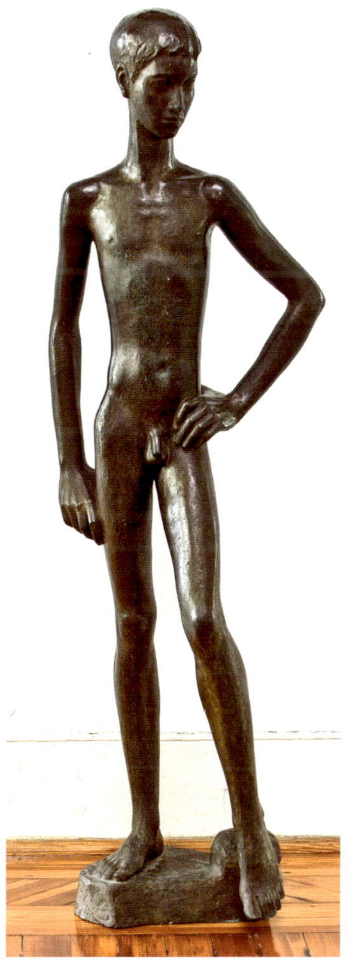

Fig. 74. Willard Hirsch, *The Stripling*, 1930s. Bronze, 4 ft. tall, Hirsch family collection. Photo by Douglas M. Pinkerton.

muscles or the clavicle in any science course but instead from his efforts to instruct me in the correct presentation of the upper body. He generally preferred human figures to be in action, but if you got that far along you began by making "kouros" figures to learn the correct proportions and then put them into motion afterwards. There was one iron-clad rule that had to be followed: anything that you were trying to fashion had to be a living and mobile creature of some kind—no ashtrays, or bowls, or trees, or little houses. If he spotted anyone deviating from the rule, the penalty was swift and harsh. He would simply walk over and smash whatever it was with one emphatic gesture of his hand. This was followed by a proclamation of the rule, "No ashtrays! It must be alive! Start over! Make something with some life in it!"

Mr. Hirsch was never reluctant to show us how to do something in addition to describing how to do it. This could turn out two ways. Sometimes he would take your clay and fashion it perfectly to show you what you were trying to do but hadn't been able to. Just when you thought you were home free, he would crumple it up and say, "Now *you* do it." Other times, more mercifully, he would simply intervene and change a limb or something about the posture, say "like this," and then go on to someone else.

Those classes were a great pleasure to me, and I gained enough facility to receive further instruction, outside of school, with classes that included adults. This enabled me to get to know Mr. Hirsch much better, and he befriended me in important ways. I became more familiar with the variety of his work, including beautiful and tender portraits of his young children that he kept in his studio, and he talked to me more about art. I recall his fondness for the great Italian sculptor Donatello, who I think was an important influence on his own development. He encouraged me to undertake more sophisticated kinds of modeling than I had done up to that time, including a portrait bust of my older brother, which is still in our family. He treated me like an adult and would talk to me about what I would do with my future.

When it came time for me to go off to college, he wrote a letter of recommendation for me to the University of the South at Sewanee, Tennessee. I did not understand at the time how much weight the letter undoubtedly carried. The vice chancellor then was Edward McCrady of Charleston, who was himself possessed of artistic gifts and was a friend of Mr. Hirsch; he helped design the school's All Saints' Chapel. Mr. Hirsch had several statues in the chapel, Including *St. Peter (Figure 75)* and *St. Paul (Figure 76).* My academic record at the Gaud School was, let us say, uneven, and I always thought that Mr. Hirsch's letter helped me gain admission.

This turned out to be important, for my experience at Sewanee was most fortunate. Sculpture was put aside, for there was no instruction there, but I gained a love of literature, as well as art, that led to graduate study and a subsequent long and rewarding career in English at the College of Charleston. But I never left art, or the influence of Mr. Hirsch behind.

When I was given my first sabbatical leave by the College, I was able to travel to Europe with my wife and two young children. We spent several weeks of our trip in Florence, Italy, where I thought often of Mr. Hirsch. One afternoon, after we visited the Bargello Palace, which displays many pieces by Donatello, I decided to write to him. In that letter, I thanked him for inspiring in me the love of art that had propelled me to take a trip that benefited my family and transformed my teaching and career. Not many years after that, I began to take students from the College on study-abroad trips to Italy. There were sixteen trips with several hundred students, and in an important sense the genesis of those trips lay in the studio off of East Bay Street where I first, as a boy, encountered Mr. Hirsch.

Later, I learned from his daughter, Jane, that her father had brought her my letter and expressed his happiness at having heard from me. He died before I spoke to him again. I am glad I wrote that letter, but it was small recompense for the individual who had taught me so much, helped in so many ways in my education, and so influenced my subsequent career.

Joseph Harrison, a retired English professor at the College of Charleston, was surprised that Willard Hirsch had no desire to travel to Europe, specifically Italy, to see the magnificent art there. But Hirsch sometimes explained, "That's what pictures are for."

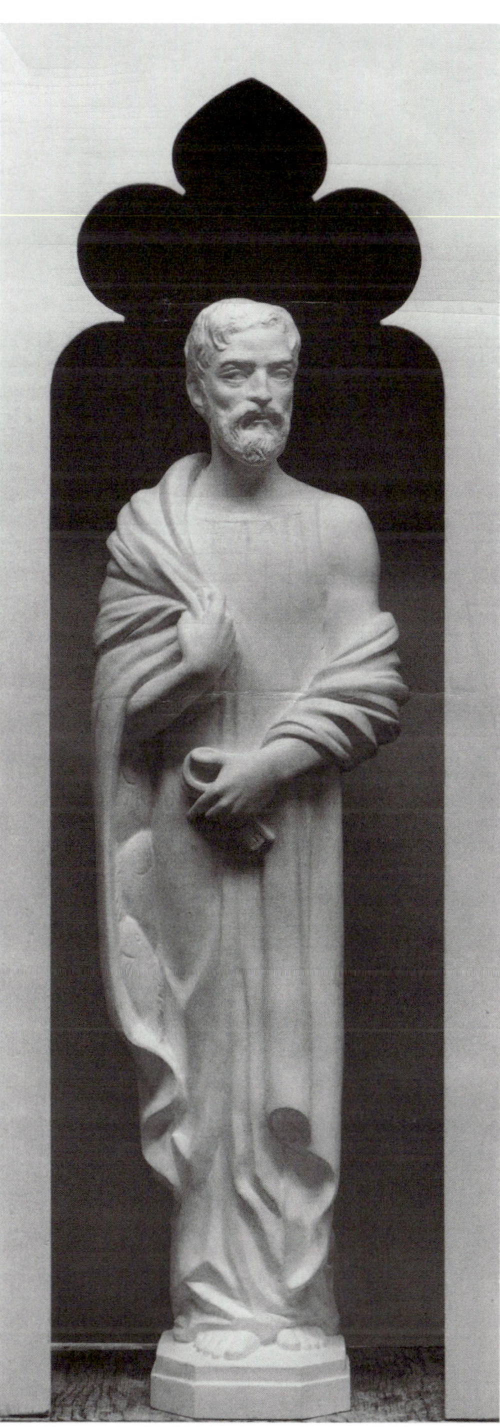

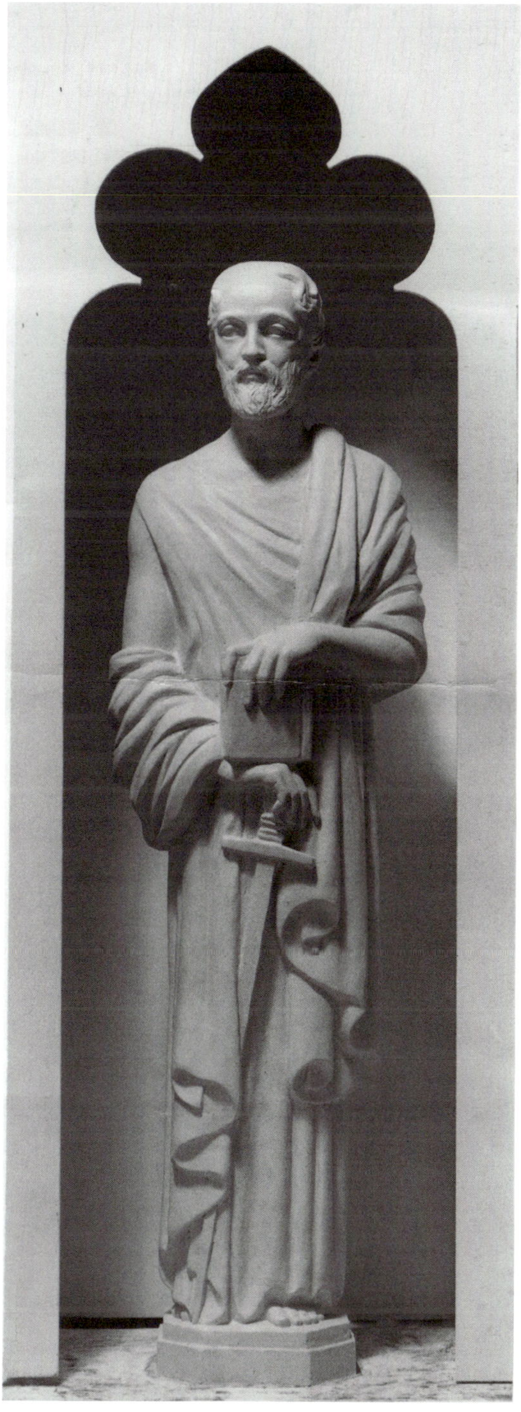

Fig. 75. (right) Willard Hirsch, *St. Peter,* 1961. Limestone, 30 in. tall, All Saints' Chapel, University of the South, Sewanee, Tenn. Photo by Louis Schwartz.

Fig. 76. (far right) Willard Hirsch, *St. Paul,* 1961. Limestone, 30 in. tall, All Saints' Chapel, University of the South, Sewanee, Tenn. Photo by Louis Schwartz.

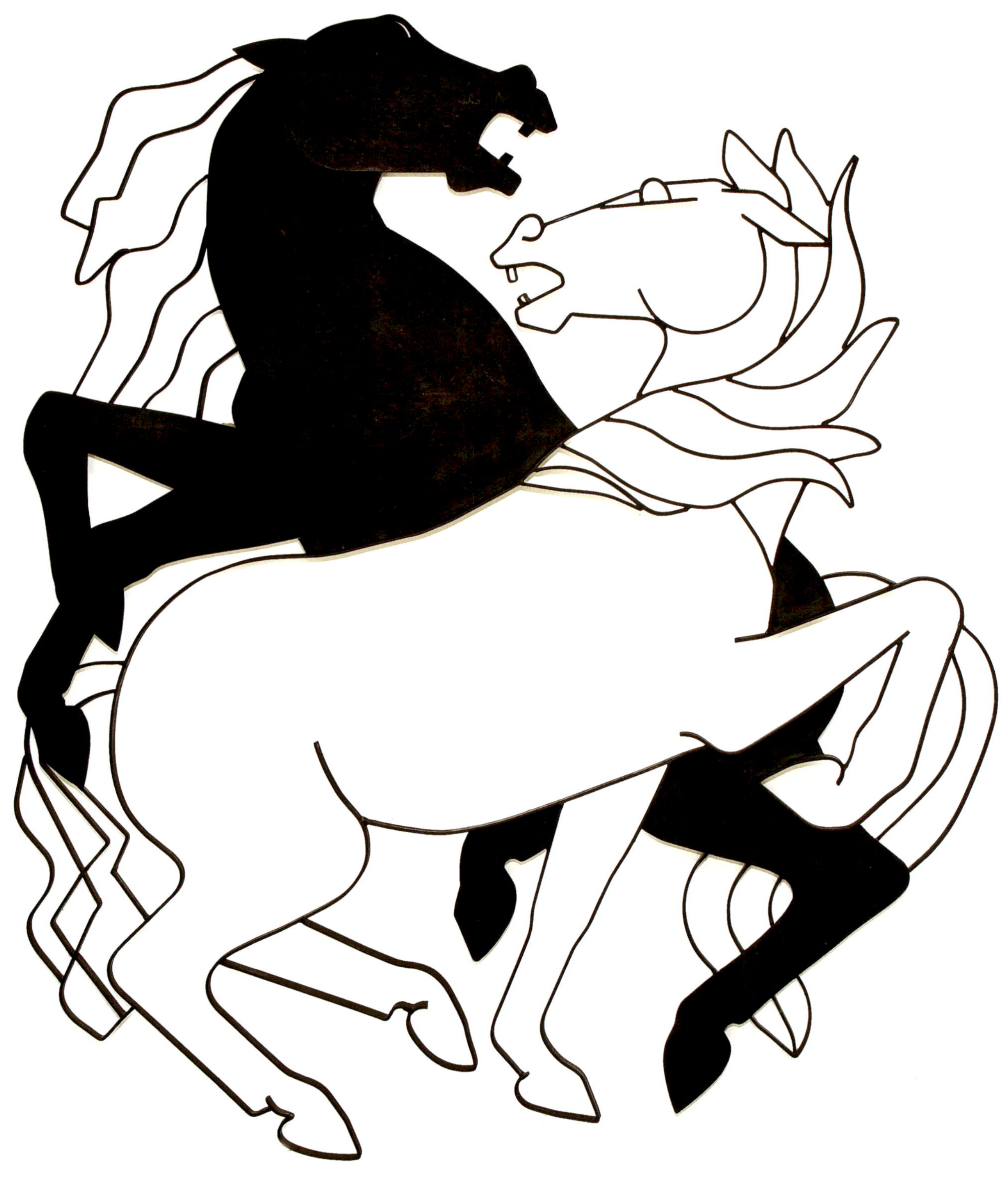

Fig. 77. Willard Hirsch, *Fighting Stallions*, n.d. Steel, 3 ft. tall X 4 ft. wide, Jack and Florence Kurtz collection. Photo by Douglas M. Pinkerton.

List of Figures

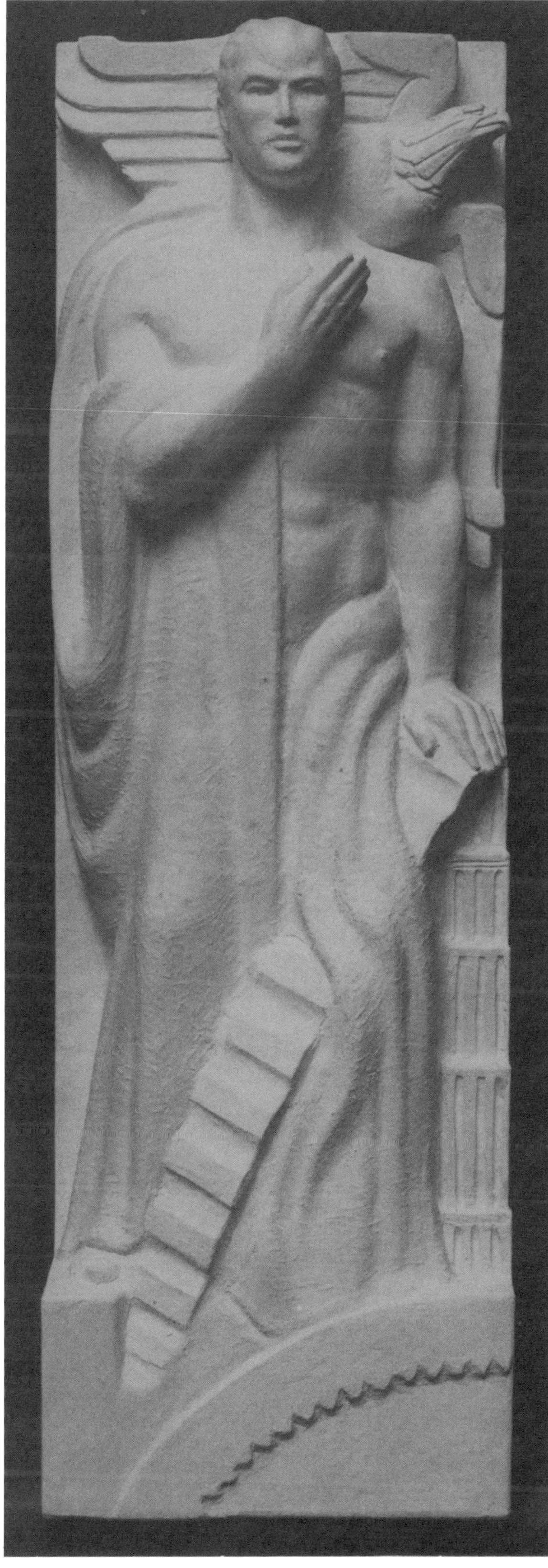

Fig. 78. Willard Hirsch, Design for Federal project, n.d. Photo from Special Collections, Marlene and Nathan Addlestone Library, College of Charleston.

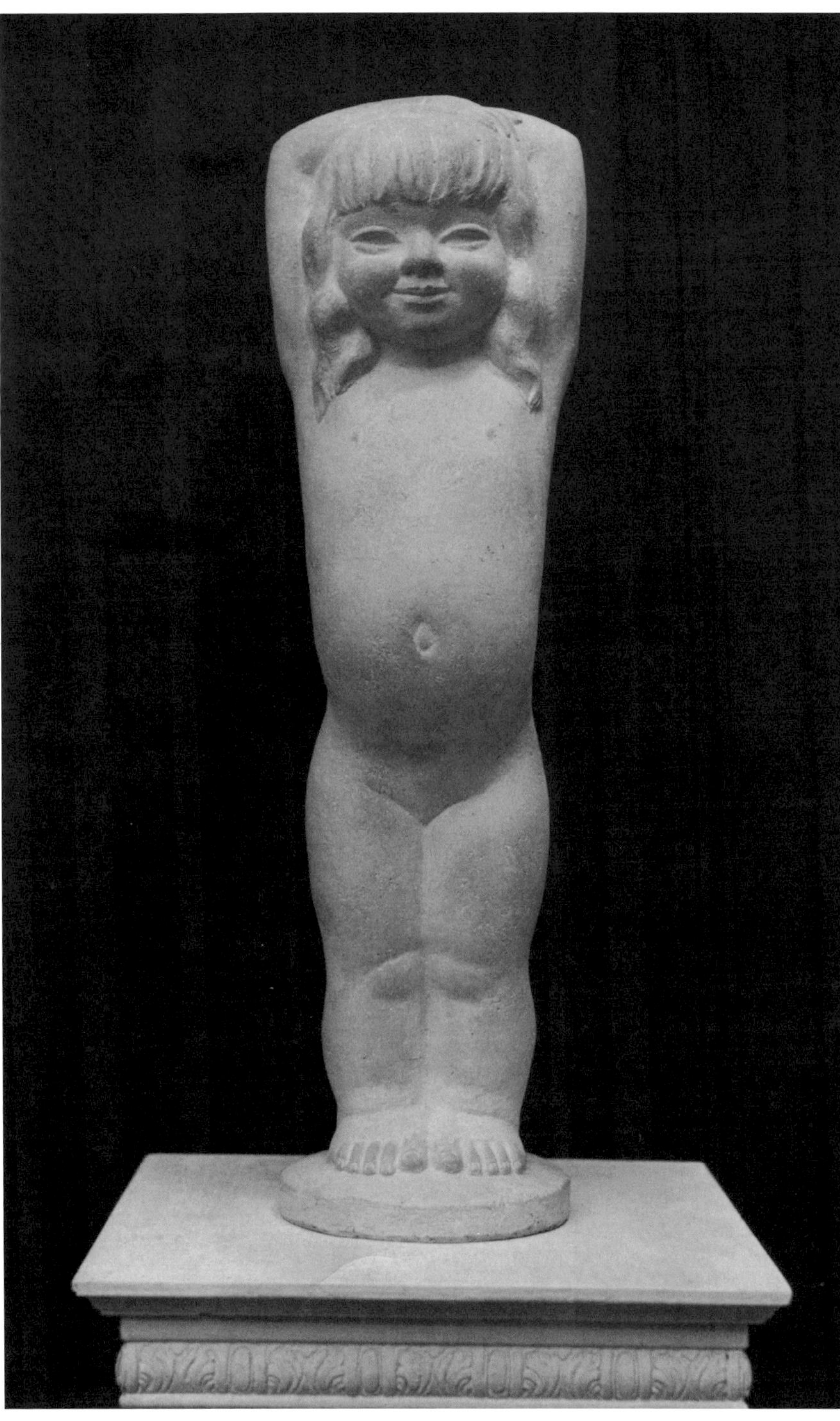

Fig. 79. Willard Hirsch, *Child with raised arms*, n.d. Photo from Special Collections, Marlene and Nathan Addlestone Library, College of Charleston.

Figure 13. Willard Hirsch, *Readers*, 1961. Stainless steel, 6 ft. 4 wide in. X 4 ft. 8 in. tall, Charleston County Public Library, Charleston, S.C. Photo by Douglas M. Pinkerton.

Figure 14. Willard Hirsch, *Alice in Wonderland*, 1961. Stainless steel, 7 ft. wide X 3 ft. 6 in. tall, Charleston County Public Library, Charleston, S.C. Photo by Douglas M. Pinkerton.

Figure 15. Willard Hirsch, *Cassique of Kiawah*, 1971-72. Bronze, 8½ ft. tall, Charlestowne Landing, Charleston, S.C. Photo by Douglas M. Pinkerton.

Figure 16. Willard Hirsch, *Lucius Mendel Rivers*, 1971. Bronze, 30½ in. tall, Charleston County Office Building, Charleston, S.C. Photo by Douglas M. Pinkerton.

Figure 17. Willard Hirsch, *Albert Simons*, 1978. Bronze, 24½ in. tall, Albert Simons Fine Arts Building, College of Charleston, Charleston, S.C. Photo by Douglas M. Pinkerton.

Figure 18. Willard Hirsch, Child's head, n.d. Terra-cotta, 9½ in. tall, private collection. Photo by Douglas M. Pinkerton.

Figure 19. Willard Hirsch, Child's head, n.d. Terra-cotta, 8 3/4 in. tall, private collection. Photo by Douglas M. Pinkerton.

Figure 20. Willard Hirsch, *Little Dancer*, 1950s. Bronze, 22 in. tall, White Point Garden, Charleston, S.C. Photo by Douglas M. Pinkerton.

Figure 21. Willard Hirsch, *Falling Angel*, 1980. Bronze, 22 in. tall, Gibbes Museum of Art, Charleston, S.C. Photo by Douglas M. Pinkerton.

Figure 22. Willard Hirsch, *Do-Si-Do*, 1981. Bronze, 22 in. tall, Washington Square Park, Charleston, S.C. Photo by Douglas M. Pinkerton.

Figure 23. Willard Hirsch, *Joy of Motherhood*, 1970. Bronze, 29½ in. tall X 56 in. wide X 15 in. deep. Brookgreen Gardens, Murrells Inlet, S.C. Photo by Douglas M. Pinkerton.

Figure 24. The Hirsch siblings, 1917. Hirsch family collection.

Figure 25. Willard Hirsch, *Chinese Boy*, late 1930s. Terra-cotta, 9 ¾ in. tall X 9 in. wide, private collection. Photo by Douglas M. Pinkerton.

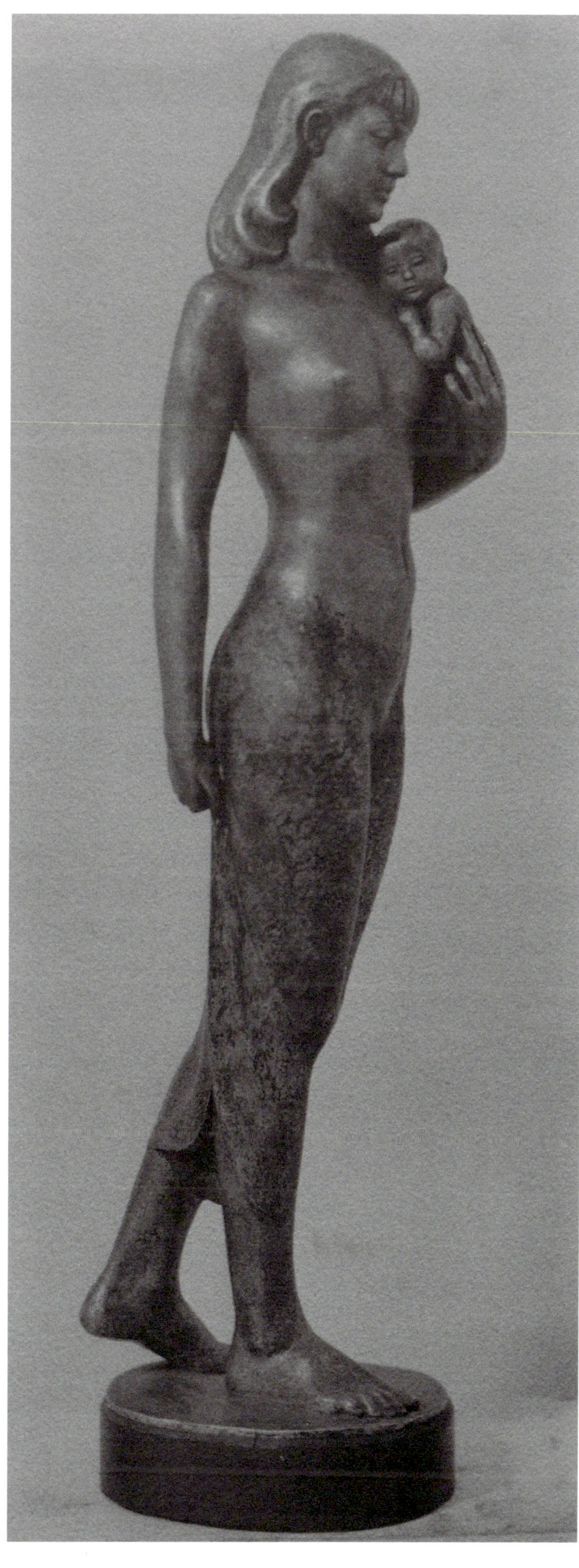

Fig. 80. Willard Hirsch, *Standing Mother with Child*, n.d. Photo from Special Collections, Marlene and Nathan Addlestone Library, College of Charleston.

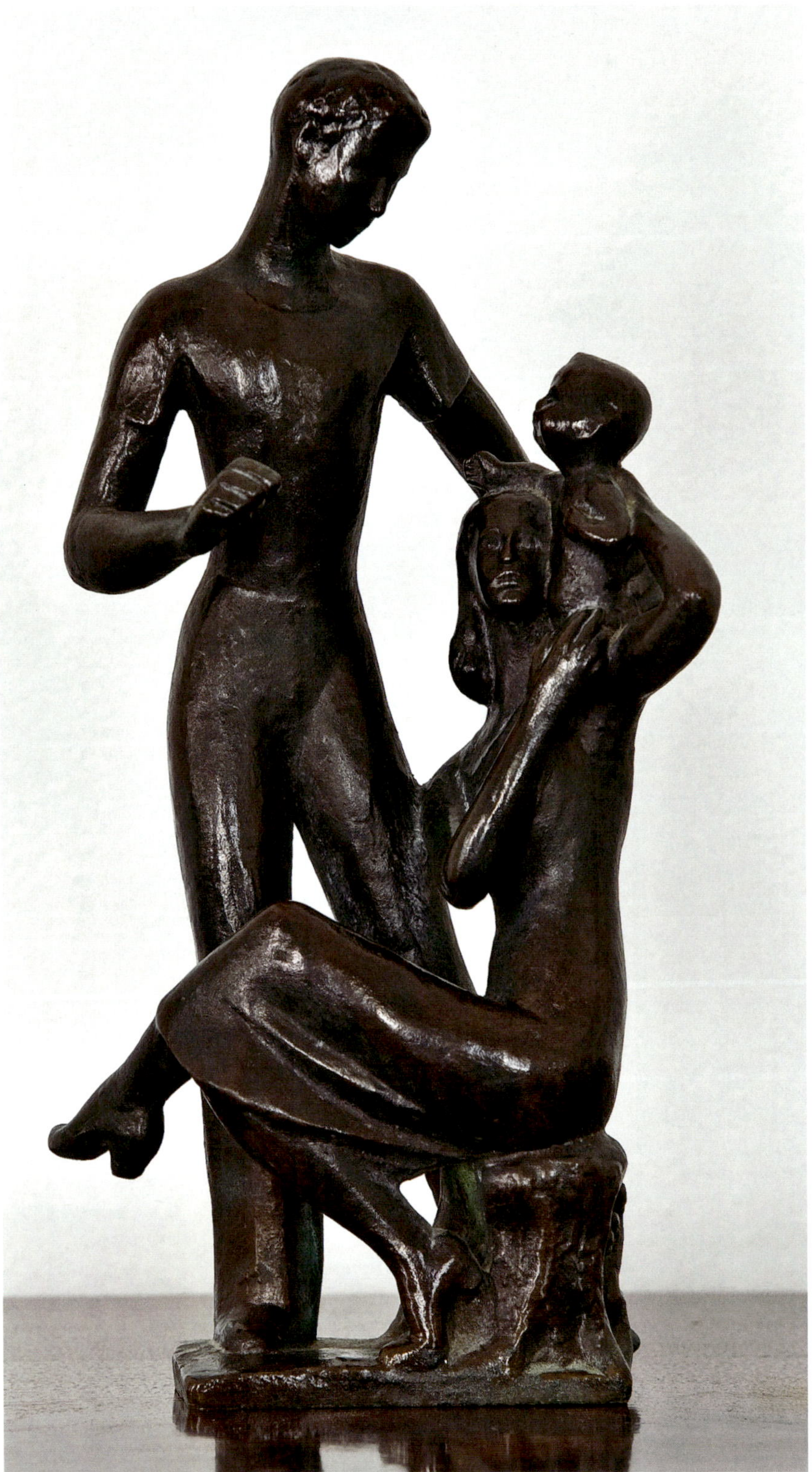

Fig. 81. Willard Hirsch, *Family*, n.d. Bronze, 11 ½ in. tall, 7 in. wide. Douglas M. and Barbara Pinkerton collection. Douglas M. and Barbara Pinkerton collection. Photo by Douglas M. Pinkerton.

Figure 38. Willard Hirsch, 1979. Hirsch family collection.

Figure 39. Willard Hirsch, *Tennis Players*, 1942. Bronze, 36 in. tall, location unknown.

Figure 40. Willard Hirsch, *Sandlot Scrubs*, 1942. Walnut, 24 in. tall, Bank of America headquarters, Columbia, South Carolina. Photo by Douglas M. Pinkerton.

Figure 41. Willard Hirsch, *Bear Family*, n.d. Terra-cotta, 20 in. tall, Office of the Bureau of Child Guidance, New York City. Photo by Louis Schwartz.

Figure 42. Willard Hirsch, National Guard Armory bas relief, 1953. Composite stone, 4 ft. tall X 7 ft. wide. Photo by Louis Schwartz.

Figure 43. Willard Hirsch, *Jonah*, n.d. Steel and wrought iron, 36 in. tall, Hirsch family collection. Photo by Douglas M. Pinkerton.

Figure 44. Willard Hirsch, *Jacob's Dream*, 1949. Planewood, 27 in. tall, Columbia Museum of Art, Columbia, S.C. Photo by Louis Schwartz.

Figure 45. Willard Hirsch, *Bulldog*, 1977. Bronze, 21 in. tall X 31 in. long, South Carolina State University, Orangeburg, S.C. Photo by Douglas M. Pinkerton.

Figure 46. Willard Hirsch, *Angel Mother*, 1967. Terra-cotta, 9 in. long, Hirsch family collection. Photo by Douglas M. Pinkerton.

Figure 47. Willard Hirsch, *Dancing Angels*, 1967. Terra-cotta, 15 in. tall, Hirsch family collection. Photo by Douglas M. Pinkerton.

Figure 48. Willard Hirsch, *The Little Angel*, 1967. Bronze, 20 in. tall, Ashley Hall School, Charleston, S.C. Photo by Douglas M. Pinkerton.

Figure 49. Willard Hirsch, *Maternity #3*. Terra-cotta, 6 in. tall, Jack and Florence Kurtz Collection. Photo by Douglas M. Pinkerton.

Figure 50. Willard Hirsch, *Maternity #4*. Terra-cotta, 7 in. tall, Hirsch family collection. Photo by Douglas M. Pinkerton.

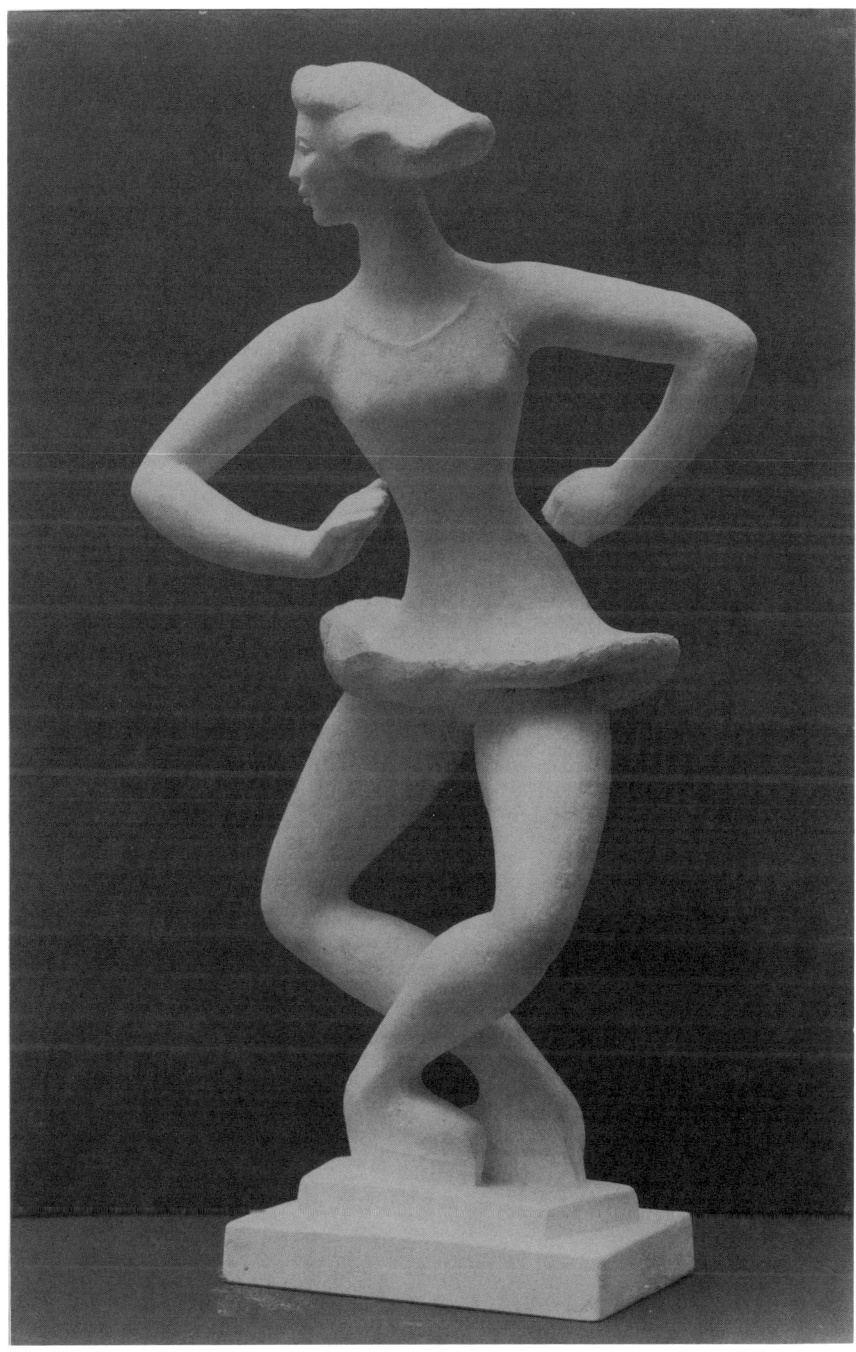

Fig. 82. Willard Hirsch, *Dancer*, n.d. Photo from Special Collections, Marlene and Nathan Addlestone Library, College of Charleston.

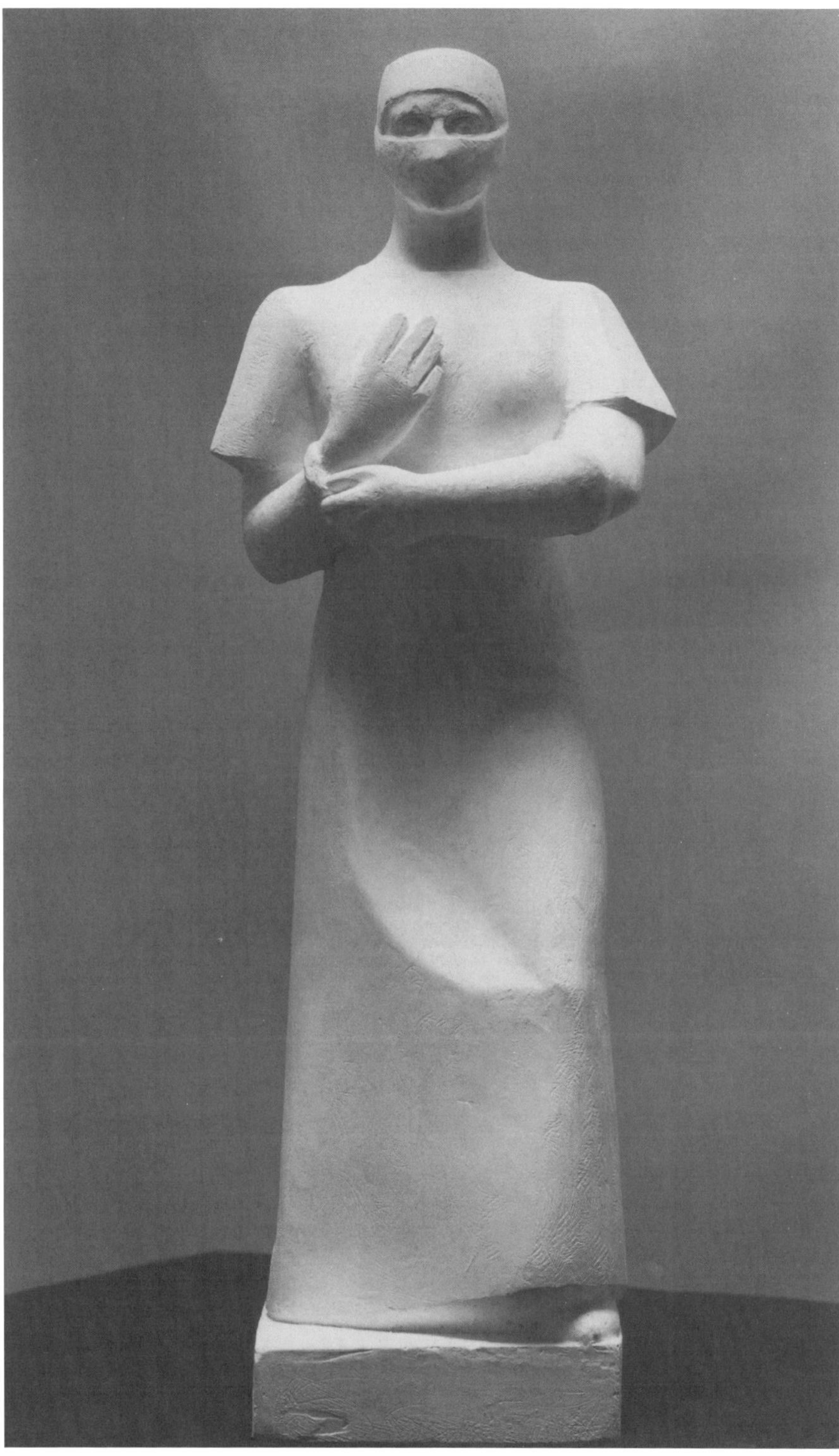

Fig. 83. Willard Hirsch, *Health care professional*, n.d. Photo from Special Collections, Marlene and Nathan Addlestone Library, College of Charleston.

Figure 63. Willard Hirsch, model for *Cassique of Kiawah*, 1970. Plaster, 26 in. tall, Hirsch family collection. Photo by Douglas M. Pinkerton.

Figure 64. Willard Hirsch, *Bull and Retort*, 1955. Stainless steel, 7 ft. tall X 8 ft. wide, Plant and Animal Science Building, Clemson University, Clemson, S.C. Photo by Douglas M. Pinkerton.

Figure 65. Willard Hirsch, *Bachman Sparrow*, 1973. Aluminum, 10 ft. tall, Alumni Music Building, Newberry College, Newberry, S.C. Photo by Douglas M. Pinkerton.

Figure 66. Willard Hirsch, *Dr. John Bachman*, 1974. Bronze, Lenora McClurg Center for Teaching and Learning, Newberry College, Newberry, S.C. Photo by Douglas M. Pinkerton.

Figure 67. Willard Hirsch, *Saul Alexander*, 1962. Bronze, 29 in. tall X 34 in. wide, Charleston County Public Library, Charleston, S.C. Photo by Douglas M. Pinkerton.

Figure 68. Willard Hirsch, *Robert E. McNair*, 1974. Bronze, 24½ in. tall X 19 in. wide, McNair Science Building, Francis Marion College, Florence, S.C. Photo by Louis Schwartz.

Figure 69. Willard Hirsch, *Leon Banov*, 1969. Bronze, 36 in. wide X 24 in. tall, Charleston County Health Clinic, Charleston, S.C. Photo by Louis Schwartz.

Figure 70. Willard Hirsch, Model of *Mermaid Fountain*, 1947. Terra-cotta, 15 in. tall, private collection. Photo by Douglas M. Pinkerton.

Figure 71. Willard Hirsch, *Mother and Child*, 1937. Terra-cotta, 8 in. tall X 14 in. long, private collection. Photo by Louis Schwartz.

Figure 72. Willard Hirsch, *Prancing Colts*, 1956. Bronze, 43 in. tall, private collection. Photo by Douglas M. Pinkerton.

Figure 73. Willard Hirsch, *Female Standing Nude*, n.d. Plaster, 25 in. tall, Hirsch family collection. Photo by Douglas M. Pinkerton.

Figure 74. Willard Hirsch, *The Stripling*, 1930s. Bronze, 4 ft. tall, Hirsch family collection. Photo by Douglas M. Pinkerton.

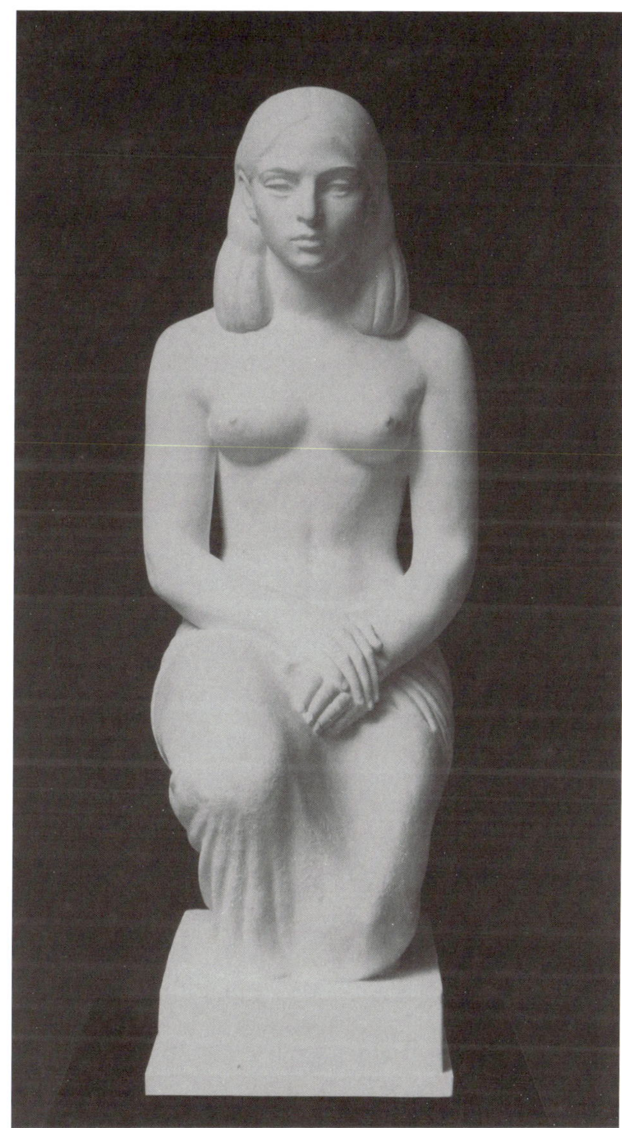

Fig. 84. Willard Hirsch, *Kneeling female figure*, n.d. Photo from Special Collections, Marlene and Nathan Addlestone Library, College of Charleston.

Index

Willard Hirsch Chronology

1905: Born, Charleston, South Carolina
1923: Graduates from the High School of Charleston
1924: Attends the College of Charleston
1932–1942: Maintains a studio in New York City
1934–1937: Studies at the National Academy of Design, New York City
1935: Takes classes at the Beaux Arts Institute of Design, New York City
1942–1944: Serves in the United States Army
1944: Moves back to Charleston and opens a studio at 17 Exchange Street
1945: Builds Charleston's first kiln
1953–1965: Co-founder of the Charleston Art School with William Halsey and Corrie McCallum
1968–1982: Uses his studio at 2 Queen Street
1982: Dies in Charleston

One-man exhibitions:
Gibbes Art Gallery, Charleston, S.C., 1942–1946, 1951, and retrospectives, 1979, 2012
Columbia Museum of Art, Columbia, S.C., 1952
Telfair Academy, Savannah, Ga., 1953
Florence Museum of Art, Florence, S.C., 1954–1967
Mint Museum of Art, Charlotte, N.C., 1957
Clemson University, Clemson, S.C., 1959
Erskine College, Due West, S.C., 1959
St. John's Museum of Art, Wilmington, N.C., 1967 (with John Muller)

Exhibitions of national scope:
New School for Social Research, New York City, 1939
"American Panorama of Art: Artists of the New York WPA Art Project,"
American Museum of Natural History, New York City, 1940
"United American Artists," World's Fair, New York City, 1940
National Academy of Design, New York City, 1942
"Contemporary Sculpture of the Western Hemisphere," Corcoran Gallery of Art, New York City, 1942
"Artists for Victory: An Exhibition of Contemporary Art," Metropolitan Museum of Art, New York City, 1942
Syracuse Museum of Art, Syracuse, N.Y., 1948
Wichita Art Association, Wichita, Kan., 1949
Whitney Museum of American Art, New York City, 1950
"Third Sculpture International," Fairmount Park Art Association, Philadelphia, 1949
Brooks Memorial Art Gallery, Memphis, Tenn., 1956
National Sculpture Society, New York City, 1961
Pennsylvania Academy of the Fine Arts, Philadelphia, Penn., 1962

Organizations:
Member and participant in annual exhibitions of the South Carolina Artists Guild and the Charleston Artists Guild

About the Author

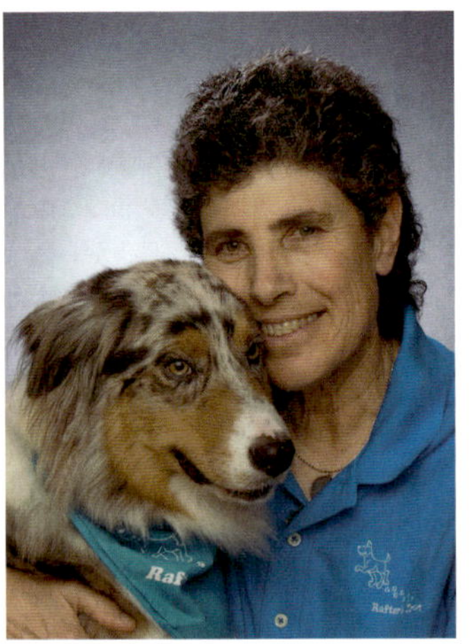

Jane Hirsch is a seventh-generation Charlestonian. She moved back to Charleston in 1999 and lives in Mt. Pleasant. Her life now revolves around her dog and her dog activities. Jane is currently the president of the national organization Therapy Dogs Incorporated. She is the author of *Rafter's Story*, an account of a therapy dog, his therapy friends, and his experience with bone cancer. Profits support the canine cancer research fund at the University of Georgia.